Maury's Musings

By

Maurice (Maury) A. Johnson

First published by AuthorHouse 08/02/04

ISBN: 1-4184-5702-7 (e-book)
ISBN: 1-4184-3728-X (Paperback)

This book is printed on acid free paper.

Maury's Musings

Maurice (Maury) A. Johnson

———PRAISE

As I raised the shade, an explosion of warm, early morning sun rays filled our family room. Flashes of bright blue caught my eye and I turned to watch a pair of Stellars Jays outside another window. They were carrying away the peanuts I had placed in our bird feeder the night before. Birds were singing their "good morning" songs and two new red velvet roses bloomed in the dew. The aroma of fresh coffee filled the air. Ah, this is to be a day of blessings and praise! An old hymn came to my heart.

> *Count your many blessings,*
> *Name them one by one.*
> *Count your many blessings,*
> *See what God has done.*

Soon, the workaday noises would take over as people drive past on the way to school and work. Our older neighbors would walk their dogs. Meanwhile, I think I got a glimpse of Heaven here on earth this morning.

Our loving Creator not only gifted us with five wonderful senses, He gave us marvelous treats to fully enjoy them. I praise Him.

> *I will praise your mighty deeds,*
> *O Sovereign Lord*
> *I will tell everyone that You alone*
> *Are just and good. (Psa. 71:16)*

#   #   #   #

3

————FRIENDS

I got to thinking the other day about friends. I'm very fortunate to have a great many friends. People who I can count on and who can count on me,—true friends.

God chose some friends who would be real losers in my book. Take David, for instance, a womanizer with a huge harem who made his neighbor's wife pregnant, then he had her husband lead an advanced patrol where he was sure to get killed. This guy is slated to be King of Israel in the future.

Then, there is Peter. Here is a hot-headed guy who denied our Lord three times, fell asleep on guard duty and yet Jesus built His church on him. He will be ruler over one of the tribes of Israel in the millennium.

Paul is a real character. He persecuted Christians and held the coats for the mob who stoned Stephen, the first martyr. The Lord picked him to carry His word about. An abrasive sort, he caused riots everyplace he went and left town about two jumps ahead of the posse with the rope.

If God can love these characters, He can love me, too. I'm praying for a double portion of love so I can love people like these, too.

> *Above all, keep fervent in your love for one another, because love covers a multitude of sins. (I Peter 4:8)*

#   #   #   #

4

————SHUNNING

"What should I do, Maury," asked my friend, Pedro.

Pedro is my close-as-a-brother pal and he had a problem. One of his brothers had left his wife of many years. He separated himself from family and friends and shacked up with a woman in a far state. Now, he wanted to re-establish contact with my friend and learn the family news.

"Regardless of all else, he's your brother," was my advice, "write him."

Some sect congregations are big on shunning those who step outside the fold. I can't recall Jesus avoiding sinners, however. He associated with harlots and (UGH) tax collectors.

> *And why do you look at the speck in your brother's eye,*
> *but do not perceive the plank in your own eye?*
> *(Luke 6: 41)*

Pedro is the only member of his quite large family to have kept in touch with his brother.

#   #   #   #

───GOING HOME

For a long time, Happy-Toes had wanted to visit the land where her dad was born and spent his youth, Norway. One set of my grandparents came from Sweden to homestead in the U.S. and I wanted to see their homeland. In our fiftieth year of marriage, we took a tour of these countries plus Denmark and Finland. What lovely countries! We saw the fjords but no Chevrolets.

Everybody has a place they consider their homeland. I haven't seen mine yet but I know it's there. For those of us who are citizens of Heaven, it will be a great day when we come to our wonderful homeland.

> *"In My Father's house are many mansions;*
> *if it were not so, I would have told you.*
> *I go to prepare a place for you, I will come*
> *again and receive you to Myself; that where I*
> *am, there you may be also." (John 14:2,3)*

#   #   #   #

———PASSPORT

I wasn't happy with my passport picture. I figured any official that saw the photo would immediately have me pegged as a Swedish terrorist. Maybe it's a good thing that nobody looked at it at the Denmark/Sweden/Norway/Finland border crossings. I was disappointed however, at not getting visa stamps on my second passport.

I've had my first passport for many years. It's my admission to my Savior and my home in Heaven. The visa stamp is a cross and it is signed in my Savior's blood.

> *"I am the door. If anyone enters by Me, he will be saved, and will go in and out and find pasture "(John 10:9)*

# # # #

————IN FIVE YEARS

Something pastor said during his sermon pulled my memory chain. I was taken I back some 45 years.

Happy-Toes was "all shook up." We had gotten a phone call that wealthy relatives would be at our place in 10 minutes. Of course, everyone was wealthy compared to us in those days.

We had just purchased an old farmhouse and everything was in disarray. If everything was average, one of the four kids had the flu, two would have runny noses and the water pump, which had seen better days, would be acting up. The odds are pretty good that I was coated with grease under our fourth-hand car trying to coax another week out of the poor, tired antique. Things were always interesting on a run-down farm.

To further complicate matters, my mother drove into the yard. She came into the house in time to dry my bride's tears.

"The house is a mess and the Hanovers are coming," sobbed Happy-Toes.

"Don't worry, who will know about it five years from now?"

Over the years, that phrase, spoken by my mother, has become a watchword in our household. It's often used to calm what could be a sticky situation. Instead of tears. It brings smiles, now.

About that which the pastor said that jogged my memory. He was telling about Martha and Mary.

But Martha was worrying over the big dinner she was preparing. She came to Jesus and said, "Lord, doesn't it seem unfair to you that my sister just sits here while I do all the work? Tell her to come and help me." 'But the Lord said to her, "My dear Martha, you are so upset over all these details! There is really only one thing worth being concerned about Mary has discovered it—and I won't take it away from her." (Luke 10:40-42)

# # # #

———LANGUAGE

Normally, I do not knock a person's selection of vocation. I consider this to be personal choice. I will make an exception, however, in the case of a granddaughter's husband. He is a handsome, talented chap and he is smart as a whip. My concern for him is his choice of a profession.

Paul attended a prestigious culinary institute in Portland, Oregon. There he achieved top grades while learning the cooking and baking trade. He learned all phases of the restaurant trade. I'll bet he can even tell you what wine to serve with macaroni and cheese or what food to have with Mogen David Loganberry wine.

Upon graduation, Paul served his internship at the great five-star Four Seasons restaurant in Seattle where he was offered a full-time job. As far as I know, he has just the one failing.

You see, I have had a television set since 1948 and if there is anything I am expert at, it is judging chefs. I have seen thousands of chefs come and go as the years have passed, and they all have one thing in common. They all speak fractured English. Their English is distorted by Chinese, French, Italian or deep South accents.

Stated simply, he speaks English far too well! His every word is understandable. I'm afraid he will never cut it as a great chef unless—perhaps, just perhaps I may be of help!

I was raised among first and second generation Swedes, Norskies, Danes and Finns. I can "Yah sure you betcha," with the best of them. I can teach him broken Swedish. He could be the Swedish chef!

I am awfully glad we don't have to talk to God in a certain language. He can understand broken English and fractured Swedish. The language differences that He caused at the Tower of Babel will be reversed when we get to Heaven and we will be able to understand Abraham and Ezekiel. Meanwhile, God understands our prayers in any language.

#   #   #   #

Maurice (Maury) A. Johnson

———COMPLEXION

The little black boy had drawn a picture of his savior. It was done with a black crayon and it was the Lord as he expected Him to look. Most of us think of Jesus as having a white or swarthy complexion, at most. What if I told you I think I know His complexion color! We are told about it. John, Daniel and Ezekiel all tell us!

Bronze is an alloy of copper and tin. The amounts of these elements vary somewhat and the color varies from a mid-to-dark copper hue. Most bronze articles of art that we see have a patina from natural or artificial aging. Here's how John saw the Lord.

> *and His feet were like burnished* bronze, when it has been caused to glow in a furnace, and His voice was like the sound of many waters. (Rev. 1:15)*

Ezekiel's view was of a darkish complexion also. He saw the Lord's skin color *"like gleaming amber." (Ezekiel 1:27)*

It sure sounds to me like the Savior's complexion is an average of black, brown, red, yellow and white! Truly a man for all races. That should frost the white supremacists.

Daniel, too, described the super being he saw as having *"arms and feet that shone as polished bronze." (Dan. 10:6)* The shine or glow would be because of Jesus' presence with the Father. Remember Moses' look when he had been near the Father and received the ten commandments? (Ex.

34:29,30) The skin color, bronze, however should be our Lord's normal skin color.

Burnished means polished by rubbing.

#   #   #   #

———NEVER ON SUNDAY OR SATURDAY!

Sandwiched between a freeway on-ramp and a busy commercial center is a patch of giant Fir trees. As I looked at those trees, memories came flooding to my mind. Those dozen or so trees and many more were the stuff of my youth. The trees had been on the small farm where I was raised. Seventy years ago, those trees were my friends.

As a seven-year-old, my chores were quite light. The two dozen chickens were my charges and they left me time for my favorite thing, climbing trees.

I was so engaged one Saturday when a boy about my age appeared under the tree I was in. He was wearing Sunday-go-to-meeting clothes and had walked a trail through the woods from his grandparents house. His grandparents were Seventh Day Adventists and he was visiting them.

I invited him to join me in my favorite tree. The trees had produced a bumper crop of pitch that year and by the time he realized that, he figured a peck of trouble awaited him when he got back. His best clothes weren't best anymore.

I didn't understand this Saturday business. On Sundays I knew we wore our best clothes and refrained from tree-climbing and other unholy endeavors,—but Saturday?

Of course now I know that the Sabbath fell on the last day of the week. Most people think that the Lord's Day was changed to Sunday in the third or fourth century. John tells us about when it really happened.

That evening, on the first day of the week, the disciples were meeting behind locked doors because they were afraid of the Jewish leaders. Suddenly, Jesus was standing there among them! "Peace be with you," he said (John 20:19)

We!!, there we have it, the first Sunday worship service. It began on the day of our Lord's resurrection! We can't always see the Lord at our worship service but He's there!

#   #   #   #

Maurice (Maury) A. Johnson

———HOOK IN THE NOSE

When I was a little kid, we had a cow to fulfill our need for milk, cream, butter and cottage cheese. Once each year, my dad would "take her to the bull" that a neighbor owned. I didn't know how, but it sure stopped Daisy's bellowing.

That bull was a fearsome beast and we were warned to stay away from his pasture. He snorted and pawed the ground when anyone came close. However, that bull had a ring in his nose. The owner had a hook with a handle and using the ring, he would lead him around like a puppy dog.

Israel's good king Hezekiah was having a tough time against the Assyrian monarch, Sennacherib. The Bible tells of the Assyrian laying siege to Jerusalem once in 701 B.C. and archaeology tells of another campaign after 690 B.C. Sennacherib was getting to be a real pain! Hezekiah prayed for help.

God answered him via the prophet Isaiah. Our greatest weapon is prayer, also.

> *"Because you rage against Me and your tumult have come to my ears, therefore I will put My hook in your nose and My bridle in your lips and I will turn you back by the way which you came." (Isa 37:29)*

#   #   #   #

———GRANDPALS

Grandson Kolby, one of our two favorite fifth graders, called and invited us to grandpals day at his school. Young Navy sailors, who volunteer at the school, directed us through the light, spacious halls to his room.

Kolby's big smile greeted us. The teacher welcomed the ten grandparents and grandpal stand-ins. As we answered the kid's questions about schools of sixty years ago, I noticed the great love bond between those of us there and our grandkids.

When our children grew up and got married I thought our duties as anchors were over. Experiences since have taught me otherwise.

When we plant young saplings, (no pun intended) we put guy wire stays on them so that they will grow straight and tall. For kids, those stays are parents, grandparents and grandpals, too.

Train up a child in the way he should go, and when he is old he will not depart from it (Prov. 22:6)

\#   \#   \#   \#

———BORN AGAIN?

The lady was worried. She had never had a great salvation experience with signs and wonders that so many speak of. No lightening or rainbows, no born again birth certificate. She was raised in a Christian home and never doubted for a minute our Lord's saving grace. But, she can't point to a day or an hour when she became a child of God.

Dr. Robert Schuller, the well-known preacher and author, says that there are three ways to come to the Lord. They are by evolution, revolution or resolution.

Some of us have a great emotional experience that is truly revolutionary. Others come to faith in Jesus by gradually by hearing the words of Christ. This is an evolutionary process. A third way is by resolve. In general, these people are not well versed in the Bible, but realize that they are sinners.

However we come to the Lord, the Holy Spirit enters us and guides us as we grow in God's love.

> *So then faith comes by hearing, and hearing by the word of God. (Romans 10:17)*

#   #   #   #

————PHYSICS

Of all the courses I took in college or high school, physics was my favorite. I love it because it deals with absolutes. Like other God-given laws that hold this universe together, (gravity for instance) the results of problems are truly predictable.

I'm thinking of the second law of thermodynamics. It is the one that tells us everything, whether human bodies or mountains, wears down. In the long run nothing gets better! It's the law that makes the claim of evolutionary beginnings utterly ridiculous.

When I get to Heaven, I'll have to relearn the new laws of physics. You see, nothing will ever wear out and that includes our bodies. We will be like our Lord and He defied gravity. I'm looking forward to my heavenly post-graduate course.

> *So also is the resurrection of the dead The body is sown in corruption, it is raised in incorruption. It is sown in dishonor, it is raised in glory. (1 Cor. 15:42)*

#   #   #   #

Maurice (Maury) A. Johnson

———GRINCHES

Christmas is near and the Grinches are out in full force. I am saddened by the fact that most of them are from the Christian community.

Oh, they say, the day that we celebrate Christmas came from a pagan holiday, that the tree that we use for a symbol was worshiped by primitive tribes. Some harp that the season is too commercial. To them all, I say, BAH HUMBUG!

Christmas is a time of giving, of loving and sharing. The food banks are full and a big pile of shoe boxes, full of gifts for children in emerging nations, grow on our narthex floor. It's a time when people hold the door open for others at the mall. Foot weary clerks mean it when they wish you, Merry Christmas. The baby Jesus smiles up at all from creches. It's a time when we honor our Lord like no other.

The strains of Christmas carols come over speakers in the stores and the hardest of hearts is softened a bit. Yes, we give gifts to those we love and remember that God Himself gave us the greatest gift of all.

No, I wouldn't change a thing. I would that all seasons were so wonderful!

> *Finally, brethren, whatever is true, whatever is honorable, whatever is right, whatever is pure, whatever is lovely, whatever is of good repute, if there is any excellence and if anything worthy of praise, let your mind dwell on these things. (Phil 4:8)*

# # # #

————ABSOLUTES OR RELATIVSM?

I stared at my voter's pamphlet. Should I vote yes—or no? In a way, living in the United States has spoiled us. Here, we or our representatives, vote whether or not to legalize various issues that affect us socially.

But, we who are citizens of a republic, are also citizens of a kingdom if we are Christians. We have a dual citizenship. The Kingdom of God is the one that will last forever and it's laws take precedence to us as believers. Thanks be to God that we mortals are not given a chance to mess up those laws by voting on them. They are given by God. They are the fruits of absolute truth and honesty.

> *And He said to them, "Render therefore to Caesar the things that are Caesar's, and to God the things that are God's." (Matt. 22:21b)*

#   #   #   #

Maurice (Maury) A. Johnson

——GLORY OF THE LORD

I believe children are privvy to things that adults miss. I think adults fail to experience miracles and wonders because they have grown blase' about such things. Children haven't been gone from God's presence that long.

The year had to be 1928. As I write this, that was 75 years ago. It was my first and the only Easter sunrise service that I truly remember.

The trilliums were blooming along the lane as our Model T pulled into the glade where the town cemetery was located. The pre-dawn chill had caused me to snuggle even deeper between my mom and dad in the tiny, heaterless cab. As the car stopped, we stepped down from the running board, and walked through the ferns that were heavy with dew and met up with a few others at an area with mossy tombstones.

I have no idea who the pastor was or anything that he or she said. As the service began, great sun rays exploded through the 150 foot tall fir trees. It was as though God gave us a touch of His Son's glory at that moment. That, I remember. The picture is still etched in my mind after all these years.

> *I have seen you in your sanctuary and gazed upon your power and glory, Your unfailing love is better to me than life itself; how I praise you. (Psalm 63:2,3)*

#   #   #   #

———FROGS

Frogs, frogs, everywhere we looked.—frogs! The huge grassy lawn on which we were camped seemed alive and moving. It was hard to find a place to step without crushing some of the little critters. Of course our kids, who were young at the time, had great fun filling coffee cans with them and turning them loose again.

Those amphibians were barely an inch and a half long. They hatched out in our campground lake and were following the instincts God had given them to migrate to another, higher lake.

It's hard to see how those little buggers could constitute a plague but there are frogs that secrete a substance that is poisonous to the touch. I wonder if that was the kind the Lord used in the plague against the pharaoh.

After seeing so many at our campground, I can visualize how they could be in the ovens, cooking pots and mixing bowls of Egypt. By the way, as careful as we were to clear our tent of them, the next time we set it up we found desiccated frogs in it.

> *So the river shall bring forth frogs abundantly,*
> *which shall go up and come into your house,*
> *into your bedroom, on your bed, into the*
> *houses of your servants, on your people, into*
> *your ovens, and into your kneading bowls.*
> *(Ex. 8:3)*

#   #   #   #

————CHURCH HOPPERS

Happy-Toes and I have friends who have spent their entire adult lives as "church hoppers." We have no idea how many Christian congregations they have joined and left, but they are many. Generally, it wasn't doctrinal differences that caused them to leave. Most often, it was differences with their ideas in how church worship should be done. Don't get me wrong, doctrine is important! Most Christian denominations have solid doctrine. If you can say the Apostle's and Nicene creeds with conviction, you have a solid foundation on which to build a Christian life.

Sometimes, pastors or people will let us down but they are only mortal. If we keep our eyes on Jesus we'll never be disappointed. If you find the perfect church, DON'T join it, because then it won't be perfect anymore!

But as for you, speak the things that are proper for sound doctrine. (Titus 2:1)

\#   \#   \#   \#

———REPLACEMENTS

Today's newspaper has an article about a new "candy bar" that lowers cholesterol. That is kind of hard to swallow. As I read on, it says that the ingredients are; gum from the guar plant, soy protein and rice bran oil.

Now, I am a gourmet of candy (I think gourmet is French for pig) and take it from me, candy is made from chocolate, sugar and nuts! Revisionists have been trying to change history for some years and now they are trying to change the stuff in candy bars.

Another target for revisionists is the Bible. Some authors have taken it upon themselves to make a politically-correct Bible. Are you ready for "Our Father-Mother in Heaven?" They have even taken away the wonderful title, Lord! The worst of the lot are the people of the Jesus Seminar. They claim that Jesus didn't do miracles or say what we attribute to Him. These heretics have already lost it!

> *"These people draw near to me with their mouth, And honor me with their lips, but their heart is far from me, and in vain they worship me, teaching as doctrines the commandments of men." (Matt 15:8, 9)*

#   #   #   #

———GRAFTS

There, growing in the sand and gravel of the vacant lot, were apple sprouts. Apparently, someone had thrown an apple core there and one of the seeds had taken root. As I thought about the God-given determination in that seed, I figured it deserved a fighting chance.

I brought the plant home and planted it where it had some decent soil. Pruned off all except the strongest shoot, and as it grew, I grafted several varieties on it. Some of those grafts took and some withered up and died. By the time we left, 16 years later, the tree was giving us much fruit, about 20 different kinds of apples.

Apple seedlings seldom bear worthwhile fruit. To get a tasty crop, it's necessary to introduce a scion from a known bearer. We are kind of like that when we are wild seedlings; When we are grafted onto the true vine, Jesus Christ, we take our place in God's tree. How do we know if the graft took?

> *"I am the true vine, and My Father is the vinedresser. Every branch in Me that does not bear fruit, He takes away; and every branch that bears fruit, He prunes it, that it may bear more fruit (John 15:1,2)*

\#   \#   \#   \#

——————SELF DISCIPLINE

William F. Buckley has stated that heroism is the ability to withstand temptation. The Bible calls people who resist temptation overcomers and has great promises for them. We often refer to these people as having self-discipline.

I am convinced that the second best attribute (after love) we as Christians and citizens can have is self-discipline. It is a key to greatness, whether in this world or in the Kingdom of God!

In general, not many of us are born with it, it is a learned quality. We learn it from applied exterior discipline. No, not all discipline is administered by the flat of the hand to the seat of learning, but sometimes a little of that may be necessary.

For those of us who were chosen to be parents, our role is that of responsible leadership. Children copy those that they look up to. If the people they admire are loving and law-abiding, they are likely to grow up to be like them. We call this kind of leadership positive discipline.

You see, if children grow up obeying their parent's rules, they are more apt to obey God's laws and the law of the land when they are grown.

> *"He who has an ear, let him hear what the Spirit says to the churches. To him who overcomes I will give to eat from the tree of life, which is in the midst of the Paradise of God." (Rev. 2:7)*

#   #   #   #

———AERIAL ANTICS

After I had won World War 2 and settled down to begin a family, I found I could use some extra money. That, and with the need for adventure still stirring my spirit, drove me to enlist in the Naval Air Reserve. My first squadron was equipped with SB2C, pardon the name, Helldivers. Because I'd had combat gunnery experience, the Commanding Officer chose me to guard his backside.

We would harass every Navy ship that entered Puget Sound in Washington with a mock diving attack. Starting at 13,500 feet, we would roll over and begin the straight down descent.   With metal straining and dive brakes screaming we'd level off just above the waves.   I'd generally black out at 75 feet during the pull out.

A thrill? You bet! But it was nothing like the thrill I'll get when I go UP to meet my Lord in the clouds. To meet Him face-to-face and thank Him for all He's done for me will be a mega thrill!

> *Then we who are alive and remain shall be caught up together with them in the clouds to meet the Lord in the air, and thus we shall always be with the Lord (1 Thess. 4:17)*

#   #   #   #

———REPETITION

When I returned from World War 2, I went to work in a local shipyard. Happy-Toes asked me what I would like in my lunchtime sandwiches. She smiled when I said bologna.

Six months later, a visiting fellow workman was laughing about the aerobatic maneuvers the seagulls made to catch my bologna in mid-air each noon. After he had gone, my wife said through giant sobs, "I thought you said you liked bologna!" I hadn't the heart to tell her that even the finest caviar would pale in six months.

There is one repetition that I never tire of. Our Father who art in Heaven—(Matt. 6:9-13)

——WORLDLY WISDOM

Happy-Toes and I lived on the beach for 16 years following my third retirement. Many of our neighbors were retired, too, and my burn barrel became a gathering place for the men of the spit that jutted out in the salt chuck.

Each morning except Sunday we would gather about nine a.m. to burn junk mail, food wrappers and the like. There was neighbor Les, blind Jimmy, John (crippled by a stroke), another Les, Dean, Dan, Stan (an old football player), Al (he survived two bomber crashes), and me (they called me deacon). That figures to be about 650 years of worldly wisdom.

There, seated on castoff lawn chairs, we would come up with answers to the problems of the day. We didn't care how big the international or domestic situations were, we would supply sensible answers. Of course, I'd get in a good word for the Lord when possible.

While we solved the large problems, we left the small ones to our wives. Things like what color to paint the house or what kind of furniture to buy were theirs.

When we have problems or challenges, we don't have to consult the BBBLSDG (the Bridgehaven Burn Barrel Literary Society and Discussion Group). It would be second class wisdom anyway.

> *Where is the wise man? Where is the scribe?*
> *Where is the debater of this age? Has not God*
> *made foolish the wisdom of the world?*
> *(1 Cor. 1:20)*

#   #   #   #

———KNOWLEDGE

"Two graduations this year," I asked?

"Yes," said Happy-Toes, "That will make eight of our grandchildren that we have seen graduate from high school."

We are very proud of our grandkids. Of course, they all are far above average. These two, one a boy and one a girl are just six days apart in age. They both have been accepted at a nearby university where they will seek more knowledge.

Knowledge is an important factor in understanding end-times prophesy. The wonderful book of Daniel which gives us insight to latter days, stresses that we'll not understand the scenario of the last-days until there is a great advance of knowledge and transportation.

St. Augustine (a.d. 354-430) was way out of his league when he tried to unravel the mysteries of the future. His explanations are still the views of the Roman Catholic Church and some other denominations.

> *"But as for you Daniel conceal these words and seal up the book until the end of time, many will go back and forth, and knowledge will increase." (Dan. 12:4)*

Knowledge will increase! Science tells us that all the lore we have accumulated from Adam's time to 1986 doubled in the next six years! The redoubling rate of knowledge now is 17-19 months.

How about transportation. The first time I flew to Europe it took me 10 days in a B-17. The last time it was Seattle to London in less than 10 hours. I won't even guess how long it would take Daniel to travel that distance. Just more reasons the end is near.

#   #   #   #

———ON FREEDOM

I remember back to 1940 when I got my first driver's license. Oh how free I felt. I was no longer limited by the stamina of "shanks mare" or of Barney, the horse. What exhilaration I felt as I sped along the lanes and byways.

Again, that feeling of freedom came with those first flight lessons as I was temporarily freed of gravity's pull. How free the astronauts must feel as they escape gravity for long periods.

The greatest sense of freedom came when I was relieved of my anchor of guilt. Oh, what new heights I can soar to. My Lord took a bag of guilt off my back that was bigger than that bag Santa Claus totes. How wonderful it is to be totally free.

> *"And you shall know the truth and the truth shall make you free" (John 8:32) "If therefore the Son shall make you free, you shall be free indeed." (John 8:36)*

#   #   #   #

————DANCE

As Happy-Toes was entering the School of Dance, she met a much younger friend. The friend was there to pick up her daughter and asked if HT was picking up a granddaughter.

"No, I'm here for my tap dance lesson," said my wife.

The lady was surprised. Happy-Toes had wanted to take lessons when she was a young girl, but the economics of the depression years made that impossible.

The class is taught by a life-long song and dance gal and some of the dancing grannies are 75 years young. They entertain at nursing homes and are well received at seasoned citizen centers.

Some 60 years ago, the church I attended let it be known that dancing was strictly taboo. Evidently, they didn't know that David danced before the Lord at worship wearing his high priest vestments.

> *And David was dancing before the Lord with all his might, and David was wearing a linen ephod (2 Sam. 6:14)*

Sometimes when the stereo is playing is playing a swing or country song, I'll set my reading aside and HT will drop her quilting and we'll take a few turns around the living room. I think the Lord smiles when we do.

> *Praise Him with timbrel and dancing; praise Him with stringed instruments and pipe (Psa 150:4)*

#   #   #   #

34

———TRADITION

"Tradition, tradition," sang Tevye, in the Fiddler on the Roof. Happy-Toes and I have seen several stage presentations as well as the movie. It is one of my favorite shows.

What wonderful things traditions are. They are the threads that hold civilization together, the glue that holds us together with history.

Our family has a tradition at our Christmas day celebrations. As soon as the oldest child could read, we had her read the Christmas story from the second chapter of Luke. In succeeding years, the other children did the honors. Then, the kid's spouses and to the grandchildren. Soon as the great-grandchildren can read, they will have their turn. We have been through the grandchildren a couple of times. I believe the youngest grand-daughter did her's while she still had limited reading skills. Her mom helped her memorize the wonderful story.

> *"And as for Me, this is My covenant with them," says the Lord: "My Spirit which is upon you, and My words which I have put in your mouth, shall not depart from your mouth, nor from the mouth of your offspring, nor from the mouth of your offspring's offspring," says the Lord, '"from now and forever." (Isa. 59:21*

#   #   #   #

———TODAY

I was surfing the channels, looking for something worthwhile to watch when I came across a singer of Irish songs on PBS. He had written a song based on a quote he had heard once. The quote went like *thus.*

> *Yesterday is history,*
> *Tomorrow is a mystery,*
> *Today is a gift,*
> *That is why we call it the present!*

The past, the present and the future and according to the Lord, He has taken care of all three. First, let's check out the past.

> *But if we confess our sins to Him, He is faithful*
> *and just to forgive us and to cleanse us from*
> *every wrong. (1 John 1:9)*
> *As far as the East is from the West, so far has*
> *He removed our transgressions from u*
> *(Psa. 103:12)*

Well for those of us who believe, the past is taken care of! Let's see what we should do about the future. An old proverb tells us that if we cross our bridge before we come to it, we have to cross it twice.

> *So don't worry about tomorrow, for tomorrow*
> *will bring it's own worries. Today's trouble is*
> *enough for today. (Matt. 6:34)*

Well, how about today?

> *This is the day the Lord has made We will be glad and rejoice in it. (Psa. 118:24)*

That's good enough for me!

# # # #

————BOOKS

I am told that 3,600 new how-to books were published in the year 2001. I would imagine that most of them are,— "How-To-Lose-Weight" books. Although we have hundreds of books, none of them are diet-type volume. I admit that t could stand to lose 20 pounds, but having been assailed by diet plans in newspapers, magazines and television, I am now immune to the ads, and to the subject of dieting.

I wonder how many Harlequin romance novels are turned out each year? Judging by the shelves in our mobile home park clubhouse, there must be tons. Do any of them have redeeming features other than entertainment?

Even back in Solomon's time, about 40O B.C., there was a surplus of books.

> *But beyond this, my son, be warned: the writing of any books is endless, and excessive devotion to books is wearying to the body. (Eccles. 12:12)*

———DUST OFF YOUR FEET

We pride ourselves by not giving up on people, believing that is what Jesus would do. We think of the Lord as being long-suffering and mild of temper. We want to remember Jesus' love and sometimes, we forget that our Lord had another side, a side we tend to forget. What would incur the Lord's anger?

How about child abuse?

> *"It would be better to be thrown into the sea with a large millstone tied around the neck then to face the punishment in store for harming one of these little ones." (Luke 17:2)*

How about defiling God's house. Dealers had pens of filthy animals in the beautiful Solomon's Porch area of the temple. Only perfect animals were allowable for sacrifice and some of these critters were second grade. Another scam insisted that only a certain coinage was acceptable for the tithe and the money changers short-hanged the people. Estimates of the Chief Priest's take of these activities run into the millions. This maddened Jesus and it appears that He drove these rascals out, not once, but twice.

> *Jesus made a whip from some ropes and chased them all out of the Temple. He drove out the sheep and oxen, scattered the money changers' coins over the floor, and turned over their tables. (John 2:15)*

39

If you really wanted to arouse the Lord's ire, you only had to mention the religious leaders. In His earthly days, they were called Scribes and Pharisees. Now we call them Cardinals, Bishops, Speakers and Committee persons. Jesus spent the whole 23rd chapter of Matthew berating these people.

> *"Everything they do is for show. On their arms they wear extra wide prayer boxes with Scripture verses inside, and they wear extra long tassels on their robes, and how they love to sit at the head table at banquets and in the most prominent seats in the synagogue!" (Matt; 23:5,6)*

──────DUST OFF YOUR FEET

Perhaps sometime we should get angry and give up in our quest to save some souls. When Jesus empowered the twelve to perform miracles and sent them out to tell about the Kingdom of God, He gave them these instructions.

> *"If the people of the village won't receive your message when you enter it, shake off its dust from your feet as you leave. It is a sign that you have abandoned that village to its fate "(Luke 9:5)*

Jesus is no wimp!

#   #   #   #

———SECURITY

"They did about $50,000 worth of damage," said my daughter.

Thieves had broken into our son-in-law's dental office and had vandalized the place. They hadn't found money or dope so they smashed objects and stole whatever was loose. The medical center where the office is located is rather isolated.

Hoping to prevent a repeat performance, the dentist subscribed to a security system that is monitored 24 hours a day. A break-in now will bring the cops quickly.

We believers have a security system, too. The Lord gave it too us when we said "yes" to Him. It's a 24 hour system, also. Some denominations believe it's possible for us to lose our salvations. Others believe in "once saved, always saved." That is called eternal security. This passage favors them.

> *"My sheep recognize my voice; I know them, and they follow me I give them eternal life, and they will never perish. No one will snatch them away from me, for my Father has given them to me, and He is more powerful than anyone else. So no one can take them from me. (John 19:27-29 NLT)*

#   #   #   #

———PROMISES

"About half of you will come back alive. The rest of you—?" the major told my Army Air Corps pilot cadet class in 1943.

I think of my brother-in-law hanging on to a balsa wood raft with blood pouring out of a shrapnel wound and the sharks circling around. I think about my high school buddies who didn't come back. Maybe, just maybe, Tom Brokaw was right when he labeled us the greatest generation in his book.

One thing you can say for us is that we weren't cowards. Here are some stats I came across for my part of the air war. We lost 9,949 bombers over German-held territory. Of the 82,000 crewmen in those aircraft, 70,000 died. Most of the rest became prisoners. A few escaped with the help of the underground.

It is said that there are no atheists in foxholes. I say, even if those foxholes are aluminum and at 24,000 feet elevation, that is true. Although my memory is faulty on this point, I believe each of us, that has been in the heat of battle, has called on the name of God. I am sure that we made promises to God, then. I wonder how many of those promises we have kept.

#   #   #   #

———WEDDING GUESTS

Happy-Toes and her sister, Hard-Hearted Hannah, are dashing to and fro these days. One of our lovely granddaughters is getting married in four months and the search for the perfect dresses to wear at the ceremony has begun. Having known these two gals for 60 years, I know how it will go. It is always thus.

HT goes about her shopping for a dress this way. She spends about three hours searching and finds the perfect dress, but she doesn't buy it. She comes home to think about it for a couple of days before she decides. A return trip to the mall proves the old adage, "he who hesitates is lost." It's been sold! This scenario repeats.

Her sister, HHH, has a different approach. She brings home about three dresses she thinks she likes to try on in private. The next day, she takes them back, and the process is repeated. Eventually, both ladies will find something to wear but they won't be real happy with their attire. Sometimes, I think it's a game they love to play.

The preparations for weddings assume a great deal of importance to many people. It was in Jesus' day also. Jesus was probably a last minute invitee to the wedding feast in Cana (John 2) and He had five of His disciples in tow. That might be one of the reasons the wine ran out. Anyway, He made a jar of great wine for each of the six of them as a gift. That's 150 gallons of a wonderful vintage. It must have been some party!

I'm looking forward to our Lord's celebration when He is married to His church in Heaven.

And he said to me, "Write, 'Blessed are those who are invited to the marriage supper of the Lamb.'"And he said to me, "These are the true words of God." (Rev. 19:9)

#   #   #   #

Maurice (Maury) A. Johnson

———RAG-TAG

"That was one of the highlights of our trip," said Happy-Toes.

We had just watched the start of the great Iditarod dog sled race on the TV news. HT was thinking about the dog sled ride she had taken on a trip to Alaska. There was no snow at the time we were there and the sled had wheels fitted on it. Amid much confusion, the lady musher guided a rag-tag chorus of mutts over a 2-3 mile course through scrub trees. HT appeared to be hanging on for dear life.

As an avid reader of adventure tales in my youth, I had expected to see beautiful Huskies and marvelous Malamutes pulling the sleds of the 1,100 mile Iditarod race. I was surprised to see kind of smallish rag-tag canines in harness. Our lady musher, a veteran of several Iditarod races, set me straight.

"We get our canine steeds from the pound," she laughed, "those big dogs cost too much and they eat too much. It costs me about $20,000 per year just to feed my dogs." She had quite a few. Some were in training, spares or young dogs waiting their turn in harness. Each was tested for temperament, strength, stamina and most of all, willingness to work.

Sometimes we feel attracted to "beautiful people." People that are more acceptable by earthly standards. We tend to pass over the "not-so-lovely" to court the friendship of more glamorous types.

That's not the way the Lord does it - Like the Iditarod musher lady, He seems to go out of His way to pick folks from a people pound.

Dear brothers, how can you claim that you belong to the Lord Jesus Christ, the Lord of glory, if you show favoritism to rich people and look down on poor people? (James 2:1)

God chose people like Moses, with a speech impediment, and Paul, possibly a dwarf, to hold important posts in His kingdom. What about the handsome, talented King David, you ask? Remember, David was a lowly shepherd boy when our Lord picked him!

Has He chosen you for some task?

#   #   #   #

———TO FORGIVE OR NOT!

The boy carried a sign. It said, "What would Jesus do?" He was part of a small group of demonstators that advocated forgiveness for the September 11th terrorists.

Well, let's see what our Lord would do! Whatever He does should be our response, too. First, we know that He loves all people, and He will forgive us, whether we are terrorists or not. However, love and forgiveness are alike and yet different with our God.

God's love is as free and flowing as the air we breathe or the summer sun that bathes us with warmth. He created us in love and He won't show anger until the Tribulation period. There is no place we could go to escape that love!

> *And we have come to know and have believed the love which God has for us God is love, and the one who abides in love abides in God, and God abides in him. (1 John 4:16)*

Forgiveness is free and available to all, also.

> *Your heavenly Father will forgive you if you forgive those who sin against you; but if you refuse to forgive them, He will not forgive you. (Matt; 6:15)*

So, what is the difference? Before the terrorists or any sinner will be forgiven, they must ask the Lord for forgiveness and repent! If they do, WE MUST FORGIVE THEM, TOO!

Repent therefore and return, that your sins may be wiped away, in order that times of refreshing may come from the presence of the Lord (Acts 3:19)

Even though forgiveness is free for the asking, many won't ask. The judgement of non-believers takes place at the end of the millennium. Jesus is the judge and He must condemn them all to the Lake of Fire even though He loves them!

#   #   #   #

──────PATRIARCHS

I didn't set out to be a patriarch. I had always figured they were Old Testament guys like Abraham, Isaac or Jacob, men with long gray beards. I was dragged into the role when my parents and brother died in quick succession. I had counted on my brother, although younger, to help me shepherd our tribes.

The title of patriarch or matriarch carry both great responsibilities and wonderful blessings. As the head of a great family, I see our children, grandchildren and great grandkids emulate so many of my moves and habits that I must give them something worthwhile to copy. You see, we teach much more with our actions than we do with our words. Our lives are the first sermon many kids will ever hear.

We must hold up our families in prayer. That has to be our number one duty. Then, Paul says that we must encourage each other. That is especially true of family heads, whether patriarch or matriarch.

> *Therefore encourage one another, and build up one another, just as you also are doing. (1 Thess 5:11)*

Sometimes, that takes on a monetary form. At other times, it's wisest to keep that wallet in our pocket. I also have a great deal of free advice, however, I won't dispense it unless asked. Someone once said that free advice is worth every penny that you pay for it.

So much for the responsibilities. The advantages? We get to go to grandparent's day at the schools. We get a smile and a wave from participants in pee-wee sports and wonderful hugs when the grandchildren come to visit. When grandchildren come to visit and hand you their new baby to hold, life is so sweet.

Come to think of it, I do have a gray beard. It's not long, though.

#   #   #   #

————MISTER 6-6-6-?

"There has to be a way to keep your identity from being stolen," said the news anchor, "perhaps an identification integrated in one's body." He may be speaking more truth than poetry. Two thousand years ago, the Bible told us that.

After barter, there came currency. Money could be, and was being stolen, so then came the personal check written on a bank account. For ease of doing business, the credit card came along. A magnetic strip on the back of the card contained information about one's credit rating. Now, the info, plus more, can be contained in an area the size of a period! Our veterinarian advertizes that he can make it possible to identify Dumpling, our cat, if she should ever get lost. It involves placing a tiny ID chip under the skin of Dumpling using a hypodermic needle. The chip can be read with a scanner like grocery clerks use. This method has been used for years to identify race horses and prize cattle. The Antichrist will make you have it if you want to do business. That will happen during the Tribulation period.

> *And he causes all the rich and the poor, and the free men and the slaves, to be given a mark on their right hand or on their forehead, and he provides that no one should be able to buy or sell, except the one who has the mark, either the name of the beast or the number of his name. (Rev. 13:16, 17)*

But wait, there is more!

And another angel, a third one, followed them saying with a loud voice, "If anyone worships the beast and his image, and receives a mark on his forehead or upon his hand he also will drink of the wine of the wrath of God which is mixed in full strength in the cuo of His anger; and he will be tormented with fire and brimstone in the presence of the holy angels ad in the presence of the Lamb." (Rev. 14:9, 10)

Another reason to know we are sneaking up on the end of the age.

#   #   #   #

———PSYCHOPANNYCHIA

Isn't that a mouthful? I'll bet you never saw that word before! I hadn't either until a pastor friend had questions about it. It, that word, simply refers to a belief that some people have. We always called it by a simpler name, *soul sleep.*

Some people believe that when we die, we lose all awareness until the rapture that will come in God's good time. It isn't something from the Bible, it's just something that some theologian dreamed up. Paul put that theory to rest!

> *So we are always confident, even though we know that as long as we live in these bodies we are not at home with the Lord. That is why we live by believing and not seeing. Yes, we are fully confident, and we would rather be away from these bodies, for then we will be at home with the Lord. (2 Cor. 5:6-9)*

#   #   #   #

———STOMACHS

"Doctor wanted to make sure I haven't lost any weight. I told him if he told me to gain ten pounds, I could get him all kinds of patients," said Happy-Toes.

HT has had two kinds of cancer with attendant major operations and has follow-up exams every six months. Cancer cells are greedy and take a lot of a body's nutrition. Thus, many people who have cancer actually starve to death. The good doctor wanted to make sure Happy-Toes wasn't losing weight which could signal another bout with big C.

My weight problem is a different matter. I am edging up to linebacker avoirdupois when I should be at wide receiver weight. I'm in the 200-500 pound class and I'd rather be in the 100-200 pound category.

Paul addresses this situation.

> *For instance, take the matter of eating. God has given us an appetite for food and stomachs to digest it But that doesn't mean we should eat more than we need Don't think of eating as important, because some day God will do away with both stomachs and food (1 Cor. 6:13 LB)*

"Do away with both stomachs and food?" I feel another Musing coming on!

#   #   #   #

55

Maurice (Maury) A. Johnson

————THE GRANDPARENTS OF JESUS

The Bible doesn't tell us about Jesus' grandparents but, there exist many historical writings of the first and second centuries. Several disciples wrote volumes which exist to this day. One of these, The *protogospel of James,* tells us. In the Greek, proto means before, or first. James was a common name in the early days. Here is what James tells us about the virgin Mary's parents.

Joachim and Anna, much like Abraham and Sarah or Elkanah and Hannah, were aging and they had no children. In fact, Joachim was told not to bring gifts to the temple because of his childlessness.

Hurting, he fled to the wilderness where he fasted for 40 days. During his absence! an angel visited Anna.

"Anna, the Lord has heard your prayer. You will conceive and bear, and your offspring will be spoken of in the whole world."

"If I bear a child, whether male or female, I will bring it as a gift to the Lord my God, and it shall serve Him all the days of it's life."

Joachim and Anna were elated when a girl-child was born. They named her Mary. At three years of age they brought her to the temple as they had promised.

#   #   #   #

————UNMANNED

"Look at that," said Happy-Toes. The bumper sticker on the car ahead of us at the stoplight was clear. It said: WARNING! In case of rapture, this car will be unmanned!

Sorry folks, the word "rapture" is not to be found in your Bible, but the event it describes is. It is the time when the Lord calls His own, either living or dead, to be with Him forever! The word comes from the Greek and it means a calling away. Many of us who study Bibical prophesy believe it is the next event in the end-times calendar.

A series of fiction books that describe life after the rapture is very popular at this time and has brought many to the realization that they need the Lord. It is the "Left Behind" series. The books try to describe what happens on earth after all the Christians are gone.

As I thought about that bumper sticker, a mental picture of a gigantic destruction derby appeared. It involved highways, waterways, railroad tracks and airspace as driver-less, pilotless vehicles and airplanes go their way. HT and I enjoy D-derbys but it won't make us unhappy to miss this one!

"And He will send forth His angels with a great trumpet and they will gather together His elect from the four winds, from one end of the sky to the other." (Matt. 24:31)

\#   \#   \#   \#

————NEWSLETTERS

"Tis the season—" to get newsletters. It's nearing the yuletide season when we catch up on happenings from friends who live far away as well as those nearby that we don't see that often anymore. We have accumulated a lot of good friends in our 76 years.

Some of those letters appear to be "brag" missives. I have threatened to write a dandy to counteract these. Something like: Grandma lost her dentures in the toilet and we had to get the septic tank man to try to find them and while we had the septic tank open the dog fell in and drowned and—. Then I'd scrawl the signature and get them postmarked in another town. Imagine the fun when they tried to figure things out!

I especially like the newsletters from Paul. There are 20 of them and they are called epistles. He wrote to mission churches he had started to teach them God's way. When I read them 2,000 years later, they help keep me on the straight and narrow, too.

> *And when this letter is read among you, have it also read in the church of the Laodiceans; and you, for your part read my letter that is coming from Laodicea.*
>
> *(Col. 4:16)*

\#   \#   \#   \#

————THE HARVEST

Dad picked a half-dozen grains from the top of the four-foot-high oat stem. With his pocket knife, he cut the seeds in half and examined them. If he found "milk" in them, the hay was ready to harvest.

If the hay was ready and ff we could cut it, dry it and get the loose hay in the barn before the Fourth of July, the holiday would be a double celebration. It generally rained on the fourth, but that didn't spoil the fun if the hay was safe.

We did our grain harvest in one operation but the Jews did theirs in three. The primary one was the harvest of first fruits. This was the one that was a tithe to God. It consisted of the first and best of the crop. Second, came the general harvest. It was all the rest of the crop except for the corners of the field which were to be left for the strangers, widows and orphans. These gleanings were the third harvest.

Those three resurrections represent God, the Father's harvest. The first and best is our Lord Jesus whom He raised from the grave. His general harvest is all of us, living or dead, who are in Christ. This harvest is called the rapture. The gleanings are the people who come to know the Lord during the Tribulation period. Most, if not all, of these saints will be martyred for their faith.

I'm looking forward to that second harvest. There is a fourth but it is one we want no part of!

*"Allow both to grow together until the harvest;
and at the time of the harvest I will say to the
reapers, "First gather up the tares and bind*

> *them in bundles to burn them up; but gather the wheat into my barn." (Matt 13:30)*

#   #   #   #

————CHRISTMAS COOKIES

"C'mon in, we've got Christmas cookies and I'll put the coffee pot on."

I could see the wheels turning behind my friend's eyes. Christmas cookies in May? I must be in for some real stale goodies.

I guess I'd better explain. One of Happy-Toes big cancer operations happened during the Yule season. She hadn't had time to compile the grand assortment of cooking and baking for the season that she usually did. She was due to come home on Christmas day and I knew a parade of friends and family would follow. I looked at a half-dozen cookbooks but all cookie recipes looked pretty complicated. Then, inspiration struck.

My friendly nearby grocer pointed me toward the baking section and I picked up a box of graham crackers and a can of ready-made chocolate frosting. Those little sandwiches are known now as Christmas cookies throughout our family and I am encouraged to bring them to our family gatherings.

I had to do something for all those visitors. The apostle Peter told me to.

> *Be hospitable to one another without complaint. (I Peter 4:9)*

#   #   #   #

61

———THERAPY-

Happy-Toes and I paused outside the door. I donned my orange clown wig and bright blue derby hat before entering.

Although we live a long ways from our church building, we live near two nursing homes. These homes feature physical therapy and are used by many after hospital stays to regain strength. Members of our congregation family have had strokes, heart attacks, knee and hip replacement operations. Normally, their stay, for therapy, is only a week or two. HT and I try to visit them as often as we can.

That outfit is sure a quick icebreaker. One friend we visited was recovering from a stroke and didn't want to communicate with anyone, not even his wife. After he saw the orange-wigged apparition his tongue loosened. Three hours later, his wife called and he was talking a blue streak.

Nowadays, humor is considered an excellent therapy. About 3000 years ago, Solomon told us that.

> *A joyful heart is good medicine, but a broken spirit dries up the bones. (Prov. 17:22)*

#   #   #   #

———FOOD

During the first of Happy-Toes' stays in the hospital I realized that I would be Chief Cook and Bottle Washer for a time while she recuperated at home. She had kicked me out of the kitchen some 55 years earlier. She had murmured something about all the utensils in the house being dirty. I figured she would be too weak now to resist my chef-ly overtures.

From the TV chefs I had watched cook pork loin stuffed with crabmeat and fillet smothered with truffles, I had some ideas.

At the grocery store, I was nearly floored by the ingredient price for those dishes. Casting about for alternatives, I happened upon the canned meat shelf and corn beef hash! Here was a square meal in a round can, so I stocked up.

Remembering my earlier kitchen debacle, I was pleased to get by with only a fry-pan with this meal. How easy it was to prepare a meal.

If you should find yourself in a similar situation I offer you a few menu suggestions. For breakfast, make some holes in the hash and break eggs in them. They cook beautifully there. Lunch hash is served nicely with fruit and for supper, a salad from the grocery store salad bar goes good with hash.

I believe that corn beef hash must have great curative powers because it seemed like no time before Happy-Toes stumbled out to the kitchen and took over the culinary chores.

Food is for the stomach and the stomach is for food; but God will do away with both of them. Yet the body is not for immorality, but for the Lord; and the Lord is for the body. (1 Cor. 6:13)

\#   \#   \#   \#

——TITLES

It can be pretty heady stuff to carry a title. In Merry Olde England, the title Knight was given to men for gallantry or bravery in battle. In later years that title has been bestowed on Great Britain's benefactors such as the Beatles who brought fame and tons of money, to England. Sir Arthur Fleming was knighted after he discovered penicillin.

I've answered to some titles but nothing that will stick with me through the ages. Sergeant and Chief won't be any good because we won't learn war in the hereafter.

I'm not awfully brave or gallant and I'm certainly not much of a benefactor. I am proud of my title, though. I didn't earn it, I got it with my Savior's credit card.

Saint Maury—it's got kind of a nice ring to it.

Greet every saint in Christ Jesus. The brethren who are with me greet you. (Phil 4:21)

#   #   #   #

Maurice (Maury) A. Johnson

———HAIR

It was a slow TV night and we were surfing the channels when we came across an old Bert Reynold movie. Bert had his collar open and a great mass of chest hair was spilling out. The hair would do justice to a black bear.

"It's a rug," said Happy-Toes, "I read about it in the beauty parlor." Beauty shops seem to be vast storehouses of knowledge.

In contrast to Bert's, my chest is a virtual Sahara Desert. It's the only place on my body where the hair doesn't grow. Then, I remembered!

All folk medicine seems to have an element of medieval torture connected to it. Evidently, the more it hurt the one being treated, the more effective it should be. At the first sign of a sniffle, my mother would mix a vile concoction of mustard powder and water, spread it between two pieces of brown paper and place it on my chest. The longer it was left on, the hotter it got. It was never removed until second degree burns were evident. That was treatment to cure a cold. I suspect the same treatment would exorcise demons.

I have no chest hair because Mom had boiled my follicles! If she hadn't done that, I might have been strong like Samson. I can't remember but sometimes when I look in a mirror, I think she must have put a mustard plaster on the top of my head, too.

Our Father God cares enough about us to keep track of the amount of hairs we have. However, He has less of mine to count each day.

"Indeed, the very hairs of your head are all numbered." (Luke 12:7a)

#   #   #   #

———SALT

My friend, Wes, was salt and he was pepper, too. He and his beloved Flora had supported their life-long mission efforts as candy makers at a yearly fair nearby. The profits went to establish Episcopal congregations. His work as a school bus driver furnished the means for their meager day-to-day needs.

Now, body wracked with disease and face distorted by a failed operation, he was pretty much confined to his ten foot wide trailer. Flora was in a nursing home from which she would never return.

Wes had a housekeeper from a senior assistance program who cleaned for him and cooked meals, but Happy-Toes would bake his favorite yeast rolls and cook rich, meaty stew from time to time. I would spend the entire 17 mile drive looking forward to my visit with this wonderful crusty old man. On my last visit, shortly before his trip to Heaven, he was really down.

He said, "Maury, I feel so bad. I can't get out and evangelize any more."

"Wes, who's to say that prayer and praise aren't as important as leading people to the Lord? That you CAN do."

When I left he said, "the Lord sent you to lift me out of my depression, thank you."

Wes is with the Lord now and Flora, too. Do you know someone who needs encouragement?

Therefore encourage one another, and build up one another, just as you also are doing.
(1 Thess. 5:11)

#   #   #   #

———GOLD

The mere mention of gold stirs the imagination of nearly everyone. It also stirs up greed in many. As the Bible chronicles life through the ages, much mention is made of the element Au, gold.

Some people of Israel got their fill of gold during the exodus. Remember the golden calf?. Evidently Moses said when he saw it, *You want gold idols, I'll give you gold idols!* He ground up the idol into a powder, mixed it with water and made them drink it.

Both the first and the second temples were richly appointed with gold. Gold Was the reason the second temple was completely destroyed. Jesus had foretold it. In 70 A.D., the Roman army built scaffolding around the 38 acre complex. Remember that the highest wall was 158 feet high from bedrock. The scaffolding was packed with wood and other combustibles and set afire. The fire was so hot it melted the gold decorations and it ran down between the stones. Some of those stones weighed as much as 40 tons, but they were removed to get at the precious metal.

> *"Do you see all these buildings? I assure you, they will be so completely demolished that not one stone will be left on top of another! (Matt. 24:2)*

#   #   #   #

———BRICKS

I looked at the pile of bricks. Apparently, they had once been an edging around a garden. When Happy-Toes and I bought our mobile home, they were buried in the bark ground cover. I figured they would make a pedestal for a table to hold my little gas barbeque. A friend had given me a part of a shuffleboard table that should make an excellent top.

One brick by itself isn't much good. Oh, it can be used as a doorstop or an anarchist might throw it through a window, but if you have a pile of bricks, you can build something worthwhile.

Picture individuals as bricks. With a pile of brick-people, the mortar of our God and the reinforcement of elders, a powerful structure can be built. That structure can be a family or a church congregation. The strength is in the mortar.

#   #   #   #

———ADOPTION

It's not uncommon for a ewe to die during the lambing process, leaving an orphan lamb, Neither is it rare for a lamb to die, It would seem the natural thing to do to give an orphan lamb to a grieving ewe to raise, The ewe will have no part of that,

The ancients found a cure for that kind of a problem, They would bleed the dead lamb on the fleece of the orphan and presto—instant adoption.

That explains how I came to be in God's flock.

> *Knowing that we were not redeemed with perishable things like silver or gold from your futile way of life inherited from your forefathers, but with precious blood, as of a lamb unblemished and spotless, the blood of Christ. (1 Peter 1:18,19)*

# # # #

———OVERDRESSED

"My gosh, I'm overdressed," said my sister-in-law, Hard-Hearted Hannah. She's not really deserving of that name and I explain **that in** another Musing.

Hannah and her husband, Pedro, had retired from careers in education in a big city. They had been members of a large older church there. Like a lot of older congregations, suits and ties were practically a requirement of membership. Here in our small fishing village, nearly everything is much less formal.

Of the four churches Happy-Toes and I have been members of, two were over 100 years old and two were new start-ups. If we have a choice, we opt for young congregations. The start-ups are doing very well and the Lord has us at a fifth church that is less than a year old.

Hannah and Pedro dress more casually, now and I think the Lord approves. His half-brother has this to say.

For if a man comes into your assembly with a gold ring and dressed in fine clothes, and there also comes in a poor man in dirty clothes, and you pay special attention to the one who is wearing the fine clothes, and say, "You sit here in a good place," and you say to the poor man, "You stand over there, or sit down by my footstool," have you not made distinctions among yourselves, and become judges with evil motives? (James 2:2-4)

#　　#　　#　　#

——DISCIPLES

We believers here in the good old USA sure have it good compared to those of centuries of old. Oh, many who would follow Christ in other parts of the world endure persecution, but we escape for now. After our rapture to be with the Lord, the seven-year Tribulation follows. During that time many will come to the Lord but most, if not all, will be martyred as a consequence.

The early Christians paid a price for following Jesus. Those who preached and wrote the gospel especially suffered. Eight men wrote the New Testament and paid the price. Seven of them were murdered and the other suffered a terrible ordeal.

Matthew was killed with an axe. Mark was dragged to death by a team of wild horses through the streets of Alexandria. Luke was hanged in an olive tree and Paul was beheaded. Peter was crucified. The legend says that he was crucified upside down, by choice.

Jesus' two half-brothers suffered also. Jude was crucified and James was beaten to death with a clothmaker's club. John suffered much. He was placed in a vat of boiling oil. Although, he survived, he was horribly disfigured. He spent the rest of his life in prison on the Isle of Patmos, where he received the Revelation from Jesus.

Then He said to the crowd, "If any of you wants to be my follower, you must put aside your selfish ambition, shoulder your cross daily, and follow me. If you try to keep your life to yourself, you will lose it. But if you give

up your life for me, you will find true life."
(Luke 9:23,24)

#   #   #   #

Maurice (Maury) A. Johnson

———MOTTOS

Hanging from the overhead beams in the high school multi-purpose room where our congregation meets, are banners with motivational themes. Each class displays their motto this way. After services one Sunday I jotted down some of these sayings and put Bible verses to them.

PATHWAYS TO PROGRESS. *"But the Gateway to Life is small, and the road is narrow, and only a few ever find it" (Matt 7:14, LB)*

ALL TO GAIN, NOTHING TO LOSE. *Do you want to be truly rich? You are if you are happy and good (1 Tim. 6:6, LB)*

QUEST FOR THE BEST. *"But seek first the Kingdom of God and His righteousness, and all these things shall be added to you." (Matt; 6:33)*

A GREAT PLACE TO LIVE AND LEARN. *All Scripture is given of God, and is profitable for doctrine, for reproof for correction, for instruction in righteousness. (1 Tim 3:15)*

WE CAN MAKE A DIFFERENCE. *And He said to them, "Go into all the world and preach the gospel to every creature "(Mk 16:15)*

SUCCESS IS A JOURNEY, NOT A DESTINATION. *"And you will be hated by all for My name's sake, but he who endures to the end shall be saved "(Mk. 13:13)*

\#   \#   \#   \#

———TOPSY-TURVY

"It's a topsy-turvy world," said my friend, "sometimes I think the devil runs it."

In a way, my buddy was right. Adam put him in charge when he defaulted on his job as superintendent of the world. Don't criticize Adam too harshly because I think anyone of us would have done the same. That is why God's Son had to come to the world to give us an out. God, though, is actually the final authority. The book of Revelation tells us that.

A lot of things in the hereafter will seem upside down to us also. A great many officials in the government, society and even the Church will have much lesser roles during the millennium and the Heaven to follow. Their achievements here do not necessarily carry over into our next life.

> *"Much is required from those to whom much is given, for their responsibility is greater."*
> *(Luke 12:48B)*

I do expect the places closest to our Lord's throne will be filled by grannies who have prayed generations into the Kingdom while earthly theologians rank much lower.

> *"But many who are first now will be last then; and some who are last now will be first then."*
> *(Matt. 19:30)*

#   #   #   #

Maurice (Maury) A. Johnson

——ENIGMA AND PARADOX

I am a member of a computer list-serv where most of the members are theologians,—pastors, seminarians and bible students. Most of them seek answers to what often appear to be contradictions in the bibical text. In previous musings, I have addressed some of these supposed paradoxes. For problems where the bible is silent, I remain silent.

David Roper, who wrote Growing Slowly Wise, says "there is no contradiction in God, only paradox and enigma. And the closer we get to our Lord the more paradoxical and enigmatic things begin to appear. We should expect that to be so."

One paradox that has caused a lot of debate is the question of predestination vs. Free will. Whole denominations have been born on one side or another because of this issue. What if both sides are right? That is how it looks to me. On the one hand, God has plans for everyone of us.

> *Who has saved us, and called us with a holy calling, not according to our works, but according to His own purpose and grace which was granted us in Christ Jesus from all eternity. (2 Tim. 1:9)*

There is one fly in the ointment! We all have veto power over what God had planned for us. Sometimes, we are not too bright.

The sin of this one man, Adam, caused death to be king Over all, <u>but all who will take</u> God's gift of forgiveness And acquittal are kings of life because of this one man, Jesus Christ. (Rom. 5:17 LB) emphasis mine.

Well, there we have it, the ball is in our court. It is all up to us!

#   #   #   #

————WORSHIP

The strains of the Hallelujah Chorus had died away to my ears, but not in my heart and mind. They were still singing, "Praise ye the Lord." The occasion was a television program featuring Peter, Paul and Mary plus a lovely choir.

I believe I worship most fervently when I join in the singing of that epitome of praise. I wonder how many millions of people have felt that way since the 14th century when that music was born.

Happy-Toes and I are back worshiping in a high school for the second time. Our last "high school" congregation is alive and thriving and the Lord moved us to another area and even another denomination.

As we worshiped in the school multi-purpose room, I saw no organ, no robes and we recited no liturgy. The trappings of religion were missing, but our Lord was there. The guitars, drums and keyboard led us in songs of praise. I got to wondering how many of those other trappings are necessary. I suppose they do trigger a worship mode in some people but they're not really needed for true worship.

The hymns and praise songs are definitely worship, as are the prayers of thanksgiving. I'm sorry, pastors, your homily/sermon comes under the heading of teaching as does the liturgy. I suspect that the liturgy was important before people had access to personal Bibles. Come to think of it, so few read their Bibles now, maybe liturgy is important to them. Real worship takes place after we leave services.

Religion that God our Father accepts as pure and faultless is this: to look after orphans and

*widows in their distress and to keep oneself
from being polluted by the world. (James 1:27)*

#   #   #   #

Maurice (Maury) A. Johnson

————HEAVENWARD

"He's so heavenly-minded he's no earthly good." said the TV preacher.

I guess it's natural to think about Heaven when we get past the three-score-and-ten years we are allotted. I've been interested in the subject for a few years and I expect glories beyond earthly comprehension when I get to the home the Lord has prepared for me. Here and now, I think I'll let that TV preacher argue with Paul.

> *Since you became alive again, so to speak, when Christ arose from the dead, now set your sights on the rich treasures and joys of heaven where He sits beside God in the place of honor and power. Let heaven fill your thoughts; don't spend your time worrying about things down here. (Col. 3:1,2 LB)*

O.K. Paul, I will. I will reflect on the replacement for the pain-wracked body I have here on earth. I'm really looking forward to that!

Certainly, our bodies will be completely recreated. We are told that there will be nothing in Heaven that defiles. Yes, sin defiles, but death and body wastes do too, so we know that our digestive system will be revamped. Paul tells us that, too.

> *Food is for the stomach, and the stomach is for food, but God will do away with both of them.*

*Yet the body is not for immorality, but for the
Lord; and the Lord is for the body.
(1 Cor. 6:13)*

We will no doubt eat something wonderful at the
marriage supper of the lamb (Rev. 19:9). Then, too, there is
God's orchard by the river of life. (Rev. 22:2)

# # # #

———SPECIAL FRIEND

One of Happy-Toes' correspondents sent this wonderful poem to her. I do not know the author but I would like to thank her.

> Someone needs your smile today
> Your hug, your listening ear.
> Someone needs encouragement
> And gentle words of cheer.
>
> Someone needs your helping hand,
> Your letter and what's more,
> Someone needs your visit
> To make their spirits soar.
>
> Someone needs affection
> When they are feeling blue.
> Listen, someone's calling
> For a special friend like you!
>
> By Jacqueline Schiff

————MORNING PRAYER

Happy-Toes says she starts off the day with this prayer.

I want to thank you, Lord for being close to me so far this day. With your help, I haven't been impatient, lost my temper, been grumpy, judgmental or envious of anyone. But I will be getting out of bed in a minute, and I think I'll really need your help then. AMEN

#   #   #   #

Maurice (Maury) A. Johnson

———HOSPITALITY

Happy-Toes has the gift and talent of hospitality. I believe she could feed the multitude with seven rolls and two small fishes—IF she had potatoes, too. She is three-quarters Norwegian and she gets panicky when our supply of spuds run low. I think, if she had her way, the Lord would have used potatoes and coffee for communion.

Although our circumstances were often meager, our four children were always welcome to bring their friends home and they would never go away hungry unless they were very picky. I can remember times when I thought half the musicians of a major college's marching band were decorating the furniture and floors of our home. Some of those young people are still our friends. Our Lord equates hospitality and generosity with love.

> *Be hospitable to one another without complaint. (1 Peter 4:9)*

# # # #

————ACTING

In his later years, my dad was a real joker. At the grocery store, he would hide behind the egg display. When someone came to get hen fruit, he would imitate the "cheep" of a just-hatched baby chick. I've seen elderly ladies turn away without their cackle-berries when dad went into his act. He had an ear for impersonation and his Dr. Henry Kissinger bit on the telephone even fooled me. He should have been an actor.

I have known people who "go into their act" when they are in church or talk to the pastor. Their demeanor is a lot different when they get 10 feet outside the church door. The word hypocrite comes from the eleventh century name for actors. Hypocrisy by Christians is often cited as an excuse for not attending church.

I know all about hypocrites. Once upon a time I was one.

> *Jesus replied, "You bunch of hypocrites! Isaiah the prophet described you very well when he said, 'These people speak very prettily about the Lord but they have no love for Him at all Their worship is a farce.'" (Mark7:6)*

#   #   #   #

Maurice (Maury) A. Johnson

———AMNESIA

The TV preacher said that at the believers judgement our whole lives will flash before us and give us a taste of the hurt we have given others. I'm sorry brother, I can't buy that.

> *There is therefore now no condemnation for those who are in Christ Jesus. (Rom. 8:1)*

In other words, those sins we confessed do not exist! There are very few things that God cannot do. He can not lie and He can't remember those sins. He has chosen to have amnesia as far as they are concerned. We are the ones who drag those sins back,

> *"For I will be merciful to their iniquities, and I will remember their sins no more." (Heb. 8:12)*

The believers judgement is a time of rewarding us for the things we have done that the Lord puts a priority on. The things that we have done in love in Jesus' name. God doesn't record failure and I'm sure glad of that.

\#   \#   \#   \#

———WATER

"That water is awful, It's full of chlorine," said Happy-Toes when she first tasted the municipal water that served our second-hand mobile home. I agreed, as I remembered the wonderful, pure water from the farm we once owned.

The small 20-acre farm had been served by a 15-foot-deep dug well. When a mobile home park with it's big septic system was built near our valley, I was concerned. With two coat hangers, I dowsed a likely spot and contracted to have a well drilled.

That well gave us beautiful, clear, cold, wonderful Adam's ale. Often on a hot summer's day, I have thought how nice it would be to have a glass of it. I don't think I would think to make a sacrifice of it like David did.

> *David remarked longingly to his men, "Oh, how I would love some of that good water from the well in Bethlehem, the one by the gate." So the three broke through the Philistine lines, drew some water from the well, and brought it back to David. But he refused to drink it. Instead, he poured it out before the Lord. "The Lord forbid that I should drink this? he exclaimed. "This water is as precious as the blood of these men who risked their lives to bring it to me." So David did not drink it. This is an example of the exploits of the Three. (2 Samuel 23:15-17)*

How would you like to have buddies like David had?

# # # #

Maurice (Maury) A. Johnson

———EMPTY CALORIES

I have been trying to lose a little weight. Currently, I'm in the 200-500 pound class and would like to be in the 100-200 category. I thought that maybe if I ate those empty calories I hear nutritionists talk about, weight loss would follow. When Happy-Toes told me what they were, I realized that is how I got to be a super-heavyweight.

We have visited congregations where empty calories are served. Not only at coffee time, but during the service, also. Give me poems by David, not Longfellow, words by Jesus, not some professor or lawmaker.

I do believe I've got the weight situation solved! I am now 18½ hands tall and weigh in at 13 ½ stone. You are welcome to use these measurements even if you are not a horse. By the way, a hand is 4 inches and a stone is 14 pounds.

But to you who fear My name the Sun of Righteousness shall arise with healing in His wings; and you shall go out and grow fat like stall-fed calves. (Mal. 4:2)

\#   \#   \#   \#

———MEMBERSHIP

When Happy-Toes and I were first married, we joined the Eagles Lodge near where we lived. It was a nice, very reasonable place to eat, and Saturday nights a small dance band made wonderful music. When we moved to another town without a lodge, I failed to pay my dues and our membership lapsed. I was no longer an Eagle.

I know people who believe in a partial rapture. They believe that there are Christians who are no longer in "good standing" who will be left behind when the Lord calls us home. They think some saints haven't paid their dues. This is a "works" based salvation and there are isms that embrace the idea. Yes, we do good works because we love the Lord, but our salvation doesn't hinge on our works. At the believers judgement, rewards will be given for those works.

We join God's Kingdom the moment we accept our lord Jesus' payment for our sins! The only way we can lose our heavenly citizenship is to renounce Him.

> *For by grace you have been saved through faith; and not of yourselves, it is the girl of God; not as a result of works, that no one should boast. (Eph. 2:8,9)*

#   #   #   #

Maurice (Maury) A. Johnson

———RHINO LINING

At our county fair, I was interested in a display of rhino lining. It's a product that is applied directly to the bed of a truck like a thick skin instead of a separate plastic bedliner. It truly looks as tough as a rhinoceros hide. It looks like it could shed most anything. I had it applied to the bed of my small second-hand truck.

Once upon a time, I was timid about sharing my faith. I suppose I feared being taunted by unbelievers. I had thin skin, then.

As I grew in faith and walked with the Lord, I grew my own rhino hide. On the way home from services one Sunday, I rolled down my car window to greet a neighbor. "I suppose you've been to church to try to save your soul," he said. "You bet, I sure have."

I get quite a few of those taunts and you know, it doesn't bother me one bit. I went home and prayed for his soul.

What then? If some did not believe, their unbelief will not nullify the faithfulness of God, will it? (Rom. 3:3)

\#   \#   \#   \#

———MIRRORS

I seldom spend much time looking in a mirror. Normally, the only times are when I shave or make sure my shirt is buttoned right. The other day, while washing my face I stopped and took inventory. I saw the pink hair on top of my head, the wrinkles, moles and discolorations. I guess I'll never be a leading man in films. Now that Gabby Hayes and Walter Matthau have passed from the scene, I might be able to fill in as a character actor. The more wrinkles the better for those roles.

In much the same way, we can check our soul's condition with our God-given mirror,—the Bible. Our Lord and the writers of that wonderful book give us the ideals which we can use to check our souls.

You know what? My soul has warts and moles, too! I'll never have a completely pure soul until I go through the Lord's laundry at the death of my body or at the rapture.

> *My soul waits in silence for God only;*
> *from Him is my salvation. (Psa. 62:1)*

#   #   #   #

———GOOD STUFF

Next to the checkout stand at the grocery store was a rack full of tabloid news (?) papers. The cheap, tawdry headlines were nearly enough to make me sick. They had to be lies.

When I got home with the groceries, a magazine had come with the mail. What a contrast to the trash I saw at the store. It was one of a group of periodicals that emphasize the good things.

The publisher puts out several magazines for people in the country, those of us that came from farms and wanabee farmers. Periodicals include; Birds and Blooms, Country, Country Woman and Taste of Home. They all feature slick paper, beautiful colored pictures and NO advertizing.

It was Taste of Home that came in the mail that day. There is a page in the magazine where we can ask the readers for specific recipes. I had asked for a dish I had remembered as Wilted Lettuce. It's a salad I had some 65-70 years ago.

Not only did I get many letters, I got phone calls, too with recipes. Our congregation nurse called and said she left one at church for us. Another lady who lives in our area called. Her mother who lives in Arkansas called up a recipe to relay to us.

"Aren't people wonderful," said my wife, Happy-Toes, as she read the recipes and notes that accompany many of them. "The people who read this magazine sure are. I can hardly wait to try these recipes."

Finally, brethren, whatever is true, whatever is honorable, whatever is right, whatever is pure, whatever is lovely, whatever is of good repute, if there is any excellence and if anything worthy of praise, let your mind dwell on these things. (Phil. 4:8)

#   #   #   #

———SEVEN SEALS

Throughout history, a scroll sealed seven times has meant a document of great import. For example, Augustus Caesar's will carried seven seals.

The scroll was a strip of papyrus or vellum up to 30 feet long. It was attached to a wooden spool for rolling into a cylinder. This allowed for easy storage and kept the ancient ink from fading. The seals were of wax or clay and generally carried the imprint of a signet ring of the author of the document.

I imagine that one seal was about the same classification as our Defense Department's Confidential, and seven seals would be Top Secret. In other words, one had to have the proper credentials to break seals.

W. A. Criswell, in his book, Expository Sermons on Revelation, tells us when a Jewish family of old fell upon hard times and lost the homestead, it was not necessarily gone forever. All the assets were listed on a scroll and sealed seven times. The outside of the scroll listed the terms for redemption. When a suitable redeemer came forth, he could reclaim the works for the original owner.

God gave Adam (humankind) the title to the earth. (Gen. 1:26) When Adam obeyed Satan, he lost the earth's title to him. However, Revelation tells us of a redeemer. He's the same one that saved us from hell, our sins and the grave. Jesus will open those seals and regain title to the earth for us!

My home congregation is Church of the Redeemer. Isn't that a wonderful name?

And one of the elders said to me, "Stop weeping; behold, the Lion that is from the tribe of Judah, the root of David, has overcome so as to open the book and it's seven seals.
(Rev. 5:5)

\#   \#   \#   \#

———DIVISIONS

By nature, we always want to divide ourselves into groups. For instance, I'm very special, I'm half Swedish. That sure makes it hard for me to be humble! Not only do we divide ourselves up by nationality, we use denominations to classify ourselves. We call each other Baptists, Four Squares, Catholics, Presbyterians or whatever. Our church membership is not a denominational matter. It's automatic when we ask the Big Boss to forgive our sins.

Since that first Easter, God puts us in one of three categories regardless of race or color. We are either Jew, Gentile or Christian. The latter group is made up of ex-members of the first two. When I get to Heaven, I don't expect to ever hear the word Lutheran again!

> *There is neither Jew nor Greek, there is neither slave nor free man, there is neither male nor female; for you are all one in Christ Jesus. (Gal. 3:28)*

#   #   #   #

———VEGGIES

I have a old sadist friend that is a broccoli pusher. It seems that this 88-year-old won't rest until he poisons me with that cattle food.

I know veggies and broccoli is not in the same class with peas and carrots or beets and lettuce. I spent a big part of my youth in our vegetable garden hoeing, weeding and harvesting. During the years I performed thus, I never saw one *Brassica oleracea botrytis* plant.

During the creation period God made it clear that He made broccoli to feed critters. We are supposed to eat grain and fruit.

> *And God said, "Look! I have given you the seed-bearing plants throughout the earth and all the fruit trees for your food. And I have given all the grasses and other green plants to the animals and birds for their food."*
> *(Gen. 1:29,30)*

\# \# \# \#

———ONE DAY AT A TIME

Have you ever gotten so riled up about something that might happen in the future that you lose sleep? Boy, I sure have! Some, (well quite a few,) years ago a rash of "Confucius Say" pearls of wisdom was the rage. I suspect the old Chinese philosopher got credit for a great many things he never uttered during those years. Here's a sample.

"Confucius say, If you cross your bridge before you come to it, you have to cross it twice!" Another old proverb tells us not to borrow trouble.

The Lord puts it this way:

> *"So don't worry about tomorrow, for tomorrow will bring it's own worries. Today's trouble is enough for today." (Matt. 6:34)*

#   #   #   #

————MARY AND JOSEPH

I have previously written about the grandparents of Jesus. The same second century volume, *The Protogospel of James,* tells more about Mary and Joseph. You'll remember that Anna gave the infant Mary to the Lord when she was three.

The normal marrying age in Jesus' day was 12-14 for the women. The age for the man was close to twenty after he had completed an apprenticeship in a trade and built a house, or a room on his parents house for the bride.

When Mary was twelve, the priests decided it was time for her to be married, They decided that Joseph, an elderly widower was God's choice for Mary's husband. Joseph protested. He already had sons and he figured he would be the laughing stock of all Israel for robbing the cradle. He finally agreed to a marriage and to preserve Mary's virginity.

Expecting the baby Jesus, when she was 16 complicated things. Joseph thought somebody had taken advantage of Mary and the priests figured Joseph an unfit guardian. They administered a test to Mary and Joseph to see if they were lying. The test involved drinking bitter water. They drank the water and passed the test.

It's not known if the author was the James who was Jesus' half-brother, his step-brother or not. That James was also thought to be the highly respected one who was head of the Christian church in Jerusalem in the first century.

#　　#　　#　　#

———TRUE WORSHIP

For the third time in my life, I find myself on a committee to examine the feasibility of building a house of worship. The last two have been built and are "bursting at the seams." They are highly successful congregations.

The congregation building we are planning presents more of a challenge. We would magnify the congregation mission through our building(s). There are a great many Christian congregations in our town. We have some that meet in a theater and some that meet in schools. We believe that our mission differs from other congregations.

The Lord has plunked us down with five acres across the street from the high school and next door to the community center and junior high school. Presently, we meet in the high school. We are called to a ministry to the students and also to young un-churched families.

Our challenge will be to build a building that is not out of place with the existing school campuses. It cannot overawe first-time visitors with polished wood and accents. It will be offered as a shelter in case of disaster. We will belong to the community.

The services we have are mod. The music, the people drinking coffee around the room turn some long-churched folks off. The young pastor melds sound Bibical teaching about present-day problems with evangelism.

A lot of my friends need a pipe organ or robe wearing choir to trigger their worship mode but, true worship begins when we leave the church.

I urge you therefore, brethren, by the mercies of God, to present your bodies a living and holy sacrifice, acceptable to God, which is your spiritual service of worship. And do not be conformed to this world, but be transformed by the renewing of your mind, that you may prove what the will of God is, that which is good and acceptable and perfect.
(Romans 12:1,2)

True worship is anything that pleases God!

#   #   #   #

——NAMES

I was never too happy with my given name, Maurice. My mother was a romantic lady and when she saw a French actor's name in a newspaper, she seized it for her firstborn. My brother, Merle, was named after someone on newsprint, also.

I would rather had a more conventional name. I would have liked Sam or Lee after my mother's historic family. I have accumulated quite a few nicknames and monikers in my threescore and sixteen years. I've answered to Sarge, Chief, Big John, M.A. and even Hey You. Maury has stuck with me for some years now. I did have a friend who called me Mo. I guess that is short for my name where he came from, New York.

When I get to Heaven, the military titles will be no more. However, for those of us who overcome, we will get a new name, it'll be sure to please.

> *"He who has an ear, let him hear what the Spirit says to the churches. To him who overcomes, to him I will give some of the hidden manna, and I will give him a white stone, and a new name written on the stone which no one knows but he who receives it. (Rev. 2:17)*

#   #   #   #

————MEMORY

I suspect that we all have departed friends we figure we may-or-may-not see when we get to Heaven. How can we not have tears (Isa. 25:8, Rev.7:17, Rev. 21:4) if we are missing a good buddy or a fine neighbor?

I had two uncles that I dearly loved when I was a small boy. They were very good to me. Their wives were lovely Christian ladies, but I don't think either Uncle Claude or Uncle Roy ever darkened a church door. Of course, we all know that attending church doesn't automatically make a person a Christian. If it did, you'd call me a Mazda when I entered my garage.

Happy-Toes had two aunts she loved and I had a brother that I was concerned about. My brother was in elementary school when I went off to war and I saw him very infrequently until his early death.

I hope to see you and all my loved ones in Heaven, but if someone is not there, we will not remember them.

The dead will not live, the departed spirits will not rise; therefore Thou hast punished and destroyed them, and Thou hast wiped out all remembrance of them (Isa. 26;14)

For the living know that they will die; but the dead know nothing, and they have no more reward, for the memory of them is forgotten.

Maurice (Maury) A. Johnson

> *Also their love, their hatred, and their envy are*
> *now perished; nevermore will they have a*
> *share in anything done under the sun.*
> *(Eccles. 9:5,6)*

# # # #

———DEATH

It was the day after the memorial service for my mother. I got a message that my younger brother was very ill. I had been caring for my parents for some years and had buried my dad a scant year before. When I got the word that my only sibling was dying, I fell apart. My brother-in-law rushed me to the hospital some distance away but we were too late. Three funerals in little more than a year. I grieved, in fact, I turned into Jello for two days.

It is right to grieve for those we love, but I was not grieving for my parents for they have seen the Savior and they have no more pain. My grief was for my loss.

Although works won't get us into Heaven, there are rewards for them. I am convinced that the Lord will take us home when our rewards are at a highpoint.

> *Watch yourselves, that you might not lose what you have accomplished, but that you may receive a full reward. (2 John 8)*

The Lord, in His great wisdom, also foresees upcoming ills. He takes the righteous to save them from further problems.

> *The righteous man perishes and no man takes it to heart; and devout men are taken away, while no one understands. For the righteous man is taken away from evil, he enters into peace; they rest in their beds, each one who walked in his upright way. (Isa. 57:1,2)*

#   #   #   #

Maurice (Maury) A. Johnson

———DIET

I remember when soft, white Wonder Bread came on the market. The bakery advertised that all the vitamins and minerals were in it and only the unnecessary bran was removed. We loved it. It was quite a change from the coarse home-made bread we were accustomed to. It was many years before dieticians decided that we needed the bran.

Some years coffee and chocolate are elixirs and other times they are poisons. Whole Christian ministries are built on telling the faithful what to eat. A bakery in my hometown is world famous for it's bread which is a recipe derived from bibical passages.

> *"For this reason I say to you, do not be anxious for your life, as to what you shall eat, or what you shall drink; nor for your body, as to what you shall put on. Is not life more than food, and the body than clothing? (Matt. 6:25)*

Pass the butter and pork chops please!

#   #   #   #

———AGING

I never thought of myself as getting old, that is until the other night. Oh, I knew I couldn't throw the tennis ball as far as I once did for Thor, the Wonder Dog. My basket shooting sessions with the grandkids have been shorter, too.

But, let me tell you the story. When I was young, I served in both the Army Air Corps and the Naval Air Reserve. Our main form of recreation was watching movies at the base theater. Among the stars were two lovely girls that were favorites for many of us. They were young, beautiful, vibrant and talented. I saw them both on the telly the other night. One was selling denture cleanser and the other was selling adult diapers!

I'm not ashamed of my wrinkles or my gray hair. I figure I've earned them all. The second chapter of Titus gives guidelines for senior citizens. Here's a sample.

> *Older men are to be temperate, dignified, sensible, sound in faith, in love, in perseverance. Olde women likewise are to be reverent in their behavior, not malicious gossips, not enslaved to much wine, teaching what is good. (Titus 2:2,3)*

#   #   #   #

——MAN MADE

It is hard for us to imagine anything man-made in God's wonderful Heaven, yet there is something Many of us, who are older, have thought about that place of God's reward for believers. We are given some hints by the Lord and by Paul, John and Daniel who were given the privilege of peeking into that wonderful place.

We think of the fresh-created earth before sin and the curse made a shambles of God's paradise and we get a hint of the created glories. Oh, we get glimpses of the magnificence when we see and smell the beauty of God's flowers. We "ooh and ahh," when we watch mama raccoon parade her young for us. We are awe-struck by the myriad of colors of sunsets and sunrises and by our lofty snow-capped mountains.

But, all these things are God-created. We will have joys that we can't even imagine!

> *You do this because you are looking forward to the joys of Heaven—as you have been since you first heard the truth of The Good News. (Col. 1:5)*

> #   #

> *But they were looking for a better place, a heavenly homeland. That is why God is not ashamed to be called their God, for He has prepared a heavenly city for them. (Heb. 11:16)*

My first sentence teased you about something man-made in Heaven. How about the scars on our Lord's hands, feet and chest?

#   #   #   #

———ON THE INSIDE

"Doctor and I have consulted and we believe you have a pinched nerve in your back," said Anne, our practitioner.

I had just spent one miserable weekend with my right leg elevated and warmed by a heating pad. I had munched a bunch of extra-strength Tylenol without much in the way of relief.

Before I left the doctor's office, I had a prescription for a painkiller and an appointment at a nearby lab for tests the next morning. I was scheduled for X-rays and CT scans, tests that look beneath my skin to check the state of my inward parts.

I missed mid-week Bible study but Happy-Toes went and our study group had prayers to ease the pain I felt.

Like our doctors, God is interested in the inner state but He doesn't need the marvels of earthly technology to see it. His main interest is the condition of our hearts and spirit.

> *God blesses those whose hearts are pure, for they shall see God. (Matt. 5:8)*

—

> *You should be known for the beauty that comes from within, the unfading beauty of a gentle and quiet spirit, which is so precious to God. (1 Peter #: 4)*

\#   \#   \#   \#

———EVOLUTION

Among other things, I'm a cosmology nut. Cosmos is the universe. Logy comes from the Greek and means, "the study of." Cosmology has nothing to do with lipstick or eye shadow.

Many great discoveries in the last few years have shot down the theory of evolutionary beginnings for life. For instance, the age of the universe has been established between 9-17 billion years. The age of our sun is set at 1.4 billion.

Not even the most radical, wild-eyed atheist could believe that our complex life forms could begin and develop naturally in that time frame! Yet, we have educators in our schools and colleges that ignore scientific findings and spout their ignorance.

Another old theory called punctuated equilibrium requires a universe that expands and contracts. Our universe has been found to be ever expanding. That takes care of that!

The modified Big-Bang theory is fact. Our Creator said, Let there be—!

In the beginning God created the heavens and the earth. (Gen. 1:1)

#   #   #   #

Maurice (Maury) A. Johnson

———THE OLD WAY

I was very fortunate to know both of my grandfathers. One came from Sweden with his bride when he was a young man. By the sweat of his brow he hewed a fine farm out of the wilderness and raised a great family.

My other grandad drove the third wagon for two families on their westward trek when he was only 12 years old. The family settled near York, Montana where they caught wild horses, greenbroke them and sold them, "back East". At the age of 14, grandad was driving stagecoach between Helena and the gold mining towns. I loved both of these gentlemen and I loved hearing about the "old ways".

Some people think that the Old Testament is the "old way" and has been superceded by the New Testament and is no longer important. The only difference I see between the testaments is that when we accept the blood sacrifice of our Jesus, it's once and for all and we don't have to kill a bullock every year.

Remember, the Old Testament is the scripture that Jesus read, memorized, quoted and preached from!

And that from childhood you have known the sacred writings which are able to give you the wisdom that leads to salvation through faith which is in Christ Jesus. (2 Timothy 3:15)

#   #   #   #

————LEFSE

My wife, Happy-Toes, makes a Norwegian thin bread called lefse, leffs or lefsa, take your pick. It's a soft tortilla that's made with potatoes instead of corn. Around here, it's a must for Thanksgiving or Christmas. You roll a piece up with turkey, cranberries and dressing in it like a bazooka and start gnawing on one end.

HT makes the stuff all year long. I told her that hers is rightsa because she is not left-handed but she just shrugs me off. She eats hers with just butter on it. She thinks I have committed the unpardonable sin because I also put cinnamon and sugar on mine and I taught the grandchildren to do the same.

The unpardonable sin has nothing to do with lefse.

"And whoever shall speak a word against the Son of Man, it shall be forgiven him; but whoever shall speak against the Holy Spirit, it shall not be forgiven him, either in this age, or the age to come." (Matt. 12:32)

\#   \#   \#   \#

──────THE TITHE

The young pastor-to-be and his intended, both dedicated Christians, arrived at the old pastor's study for pre-marital counseling. The old pastor threw ten dimes on his desktop and said, "That represents your income, it all came from God!"

Spearing one dime with his forefinger, he pushed it aside. "That's all our Lord requires you to give back to Him."

He pushed another to the other side and said, "Save that and you'll never be broke, the rest you live on!"

That young pastor is a friend of mine and the Lord has blessed him a great deal. It was hard for my wife and I to start tithing. We had four kids and a very moderate income. A pastor/friend suggested that we start at three percent and gradually increase the amount. We did it in a couple of jumps. The Lord has blessed us beyond our wildest dreams.

God does not need our money. After all, He created all wealth! It's all His! The giving of tithes benefits us. It helps prepare our hearts for God's love.

"For where your treasure is, there will your heart be also." (Luke 12:34)

\#   \#   \#   \#

———PUZZLES

I enjoy working jigsaw puzzles. After I had a stroke when I was 60, part of my self-imposed physical therapy was putting puzzles together. Oh, what a lovely picture we get when we put all those pieces together.

It is much like the body of Christ. We believers are pieces of our Lord's church. Each of us is a puzzle piece and the big picture is incomplete as yet. When that last piece is in place, our God will say, you are beautiful, come on Home!

For even as the body is one and yet has many members, and all the members of the body, though they are many, are one body, so also is Christ. (1 Cor. 12:12)

#   #   #   #

MAURY'S MUSING — THE LONELIEST CHRISTMAS

Have you ever been lonely in a crowd? I sure have. The year was 1946 and the day was Christmas.

World War 2 had been over for a few months and although I had ample "points" to come home, the 96th Bomb Squadron had been tapped for occupation duty. I had to wait until a new Flight Engineer/Gunner was sent to Italy to replace me.

Finally my replacement came and I boarded the USS Monterey in Naples harbor, headed for home. The aircraft carrier had been modified for use as a troopship. I seem to remember that 4500 of us were accommodated in compartments and the six-tiers of bunks on the hangar deck.

After losing so many comrades in the long war, we were reluctant to make more short-term friendships. Our thoughts turned inward as our visions were of home and hearth. Here we were in the midst of 4,499 others, spending the loneliest day of our lives.

I believe there were Christmas services on the ship but I didn't know about them. My Christmas dinner was interrupted as the ship lurched and the legs of the mess table where I was seated collapsed. My dinner and a pitcher of coffee soaked into my last clean uniform.

I made my way to the ship's fan-tail so I could breath air that was clear of the odor of sea-sickness that filled my assigned compartment. We were in the mid-Atlantic in the middle of winter.

Do you know of someone who might be lonely this Christmas? There is probably someone on a nearby military base or a neighbor who would enjoy God's love you could pass on. How about taking somebody to church with you and sharing Christmas dinner.

> *And do not neglect doing good and sharing;*
> *for with such sacrifices God is pleased.*
> *(Heb. 13:16)*

#   #   #   #

———LIFE SPAN

We get a Parade magazine with our Sunday newspaper. It's on the counter in front of me. Large letters on the cover promise to tell us How and Why we Age. A question asks, "Why can't we live forever?" The entire issue is devoted to stretching our life span.

I have news for the writers. We are going to live forever, at least our souls are! Although we spend a greater amount of time and money on our bodies, they are only the containers for our souls. It's kind of like taking excellent care of our grocery bags and banana peels and letting the contents go to rot.

Anyway, I do like to feel good and look decent and I like the people around me to look good and smell good. However, if it came to a choice, I would rather have their eternal part good and healthy.

> *"And which of you by being anxious add a single cubit to his life's span?" (Matt. 6:27)*

#   #   #   #

MAURY'S MUSING—LAZINESS

"The vet says that Dumpling is a Domestic Shorthair," said Happy-Toes.

I don't believe it, I think she is a Domestic Loosehair! She has black hair for my light trousers, white hair for the dark furniture and orange hair for the in-between stuff. She is a very versatile cat. She is also lazy.

When we lived on the farm, we had several cats and they earned their keep. They kept the amount of varmints down. Mice didn't die of old age on our farm! However, this city cat spends twenty hours a day napping.

Paul disapproved of laziness. Despite a physical handicap, he was very ambitious. His Greek nickname was in the diminutive. It would be Paulet in English, which would indicate that he was short in height, possibly a midget or dwarf. Whatever his problem, it didn't stop him from pursuing his trade of tentmaker.

For you yourselves know how you ought to follow us, for we were not disorderly among you; nor did we eat anyone's bread free of charge, but worked with labor and toil night and day, that we might not be a burden to any of you, not because we do not have authority, but to make ourselves an example of how you should follow us. (2 Thess. 3:7-9)

#   #   #   #

Maurice (Maury) A. Johnson

————PUNISHMENT

We tend to think of both Heaven and Hell as classless societies. Like on earth, both do have ranks. I have a computer friend with whom I have had a minor debate on this point. He is a pastor, and no, the point has nothing to do with our salvation. George (not his real name) says that all sins are equal. I disagree.

He is right in that all sins will put a person in Hell unless one asks Jesus to scrub his/her sin-slate clean. Here are candidates for the worse treatment in Hell!

Our Lord demonstrated that he loved the little children. He had very harsh words for anyone that would abuse the little ones.

> *"It would be better for him if a millstone were hung around his neck and he were thrown into the sea, then that he should cause one of these little ones to stumble." (Luke 17:2)*

The religious leaders of Jesus' day were the scribes and Pharisees. He railed at them through the whole 25rd chapter of Matthew. We have these super-religious people in this day and age! Here is what they can expect.

> —*"therefore you shall receive greater condemnation." (Matt. 23:14b)*

Here we can cinch the whole argument. We'll do it in the words of Jesus.

"And that slave who knew his master's will and did not get ready or act in accord with his will, shall receive many lashes, but the one who did not know it, and committed deeds worthy of a flogging, will receive but few. And from everyone who has been given much shall much be required; and to whom they entrusted much, of him they will ask all the more."
(Luke 12:47,48)

I rest my case.

#　　#　　#　　#

———SHEOL

When people talk about vacation spots, they rave about Hawaii, Tahiti, Mexico or some other warm place. Nobody ever talks about Sheol. It's a very warm place, hot really! It's a hell of a place, in fact, Hell is another name for it. Others are "the Nether World", "Abode of the Dead" and Abaddon.

In Genesis, we are told that it is down, in the ground. Job tells us that it's under the seas and their inhabitants. The closer one gets to the center of the earth, the hotter it gets. It's an arid place, no water at all, and it's dark, dark, dark.

Sheol is not a permanent home. The residents will only be there until the end of the Millennium when they will be judged and sent to their permanent abode, the Lake of Fire.

Speaking of the Lake of Fire, astronomers have found a long-suspected "Black Hole" that seems to fill the bill. That Black Hole has swallowed thousands of suns and it's gravity is so strong that not even light can escape. And it's HOT!

I'm sure happy I'm not going there!

"For the Son of Man has come to seek and save that which was lost. (Luke 19:10)

\# \# \# \#

———UGLY

We lived on a small 20-acre farm and our last dog had died of old age. Tippy had been a faithful companion to our son for many years and was sorely missed by all of us. This day was our youngest daughter's birthday and she wanted a dog—her own dog.

As the rest of the family waved from the porch, four-year-old Holly and I set out for the nearest dog pound some 45 miles away. There, the cages were full of beautiful canines, setters, spaniels and others. You guessed it, there was a non-de-script, Heinz 57 also in a corner of a cage and it was the one she picked. Mortimer was the world's ugliest dog and also the world's friendliest. His heart was as big as his body was small. Kid's can see through the outside to the heart. Wouldn't it be nice if we would?

Sometimes, we think our ears are too big or our nose is too small or we're too skinny or too fat. Like Mort, it's our heart that God looks at. Real people do, too.

Let us draw near with a sincere heart in full assurance of faith, having our hearts sprinkled clean from an evil conscience and our bodies washed with pure water. (Heb. 10:22)

#   #   #   #

Maurice (Maury) A. Johnson

———FAILED SEMINARIES

The young pastor looked shocked. I had quoted "Amen! Come, Lord Jesus!" from Revelation. He had only heard that phrase in liturgical context, never relating it with our Lord's second coming. I don't believe he had even studied Revelation.

In all fairness to that young man, he has learned a great deal since he left the seminary. Much of what he has learned since, came from the congregation's old geezers. When I talk to these young seminarians, I'm happy I didn't attend some of those schools. Don't get me wrong, not all of them are failures. If you or your offspring is called into the ministry, do some checking!

Scriptures relating to the end-days and to our Lord's second coming occupy a quarter of the Bible yet, seminary prof's shy away from the subject like it carried a plague. It is true that we were not to understand a lot of prophesy until we are close to the end. According to what Jesus said, and told us through the prophets, we are getting close.

> *But he said, "Go now, Daniel, for what I have said is for the time of the end. Many will be purified, cleansed, and refined by these trials. But the wicked will continue in their wickedness, and none of them will understand. Only those who are wise will know what it means." (Dan. 12:9-10)*

#   #

And He will send forth His angels with the sound of a mighty trumpet blast, and they will gather together His chosen ones from the farthest ends of the earth and Heaven. (Matt. 24:31)

#   #   #   #

————IN THE DOUGH

"I'm hungry for home-made bread," I said.

"Me, too," said Happy-Toes.

HT and I have different kinds of arthritis. Hers, *polymialga rheumatica,* leaves her all bent out of shape in the morning. Mine is fairly good in the a.m., but I wear down fast. HT had given up bread making because of sore hand and finger joints from the kneading. Maybe, just maybe, I thought, we can work something out.

Now, in mid-morning, Happy-Toes puts the ingredients together and I do the kneading. It takes from 8-12 minutes until the "sponge" feels just right. We make bread about twice a week, now. This gives my hands time to recover between kneadings.

We never have stale bread. I have tried to save some to make HT her favorite bread pudding without luck. I don't believe a day goes by that we don't have several of our kids and grandkids pop in and some of them are appetites with a skin covering.

"Man cannot live by bread alone." The grandkids want butter and jelly, too.

> *"For the bread of God is that which comes down out of Heaven, and gives life to the world." (John 6:33)*

# # # #

———WATER INTO WINE

We were having two couples for dinner and I went to the store to get a bottle of wine. Happy-Toes had prepared one of her specialties, parmesan chicken. She does this dish very well. The only thing I knew about wine is that I wanted a light one to go with the dinner. As I entered the store, a near-huge display of bottles greeted me. After about ten minutes, I narrowed the choice to two. One was a slender light green and the other was a beautiful blue bottle. Then, price was the deciding factor. I think I got a Pinot Grigio.

When I was a kid, the church my folks attended was death on drinking wine or anything else that contained alcohol. Brother Frost, our Sunday School Superintendent, had a demonstration where he would put a worm in a jar with alcohol. The worm died and Brother Frost pointed that out as being bad for us. Of course, one of the bigger boys let us know that if we drank alcohol we wouldn't have worms.

That church claimed that when the Bible says wine, it means grape juice. I can't believe a bridegroom would ever serve Welch's grape juice at a Jewish wedding party.

Six stone waterpots were standing there; they were used for Jewish ceremonial purposes and held perhaps twenty to thirty gallons each. Then Jesus told the servants to fill them to the brim with water. When this was done He said, "Dip some out and take it to the master of ceremonies." When the master of ceremonies

129

tasted the water that was now wine, not knowing where it had come from (though of course, the servants did), he called the bridegroom over. "This is wonderful stuff? he said. "You're different than most. Usually a host uses the best wine first, then afterwards, when everyone is full and doesn't care, then he brings out the less expensive brands, but you have kept the best for last!"(John 2:6-10)

#   #   #   #

———STOMACHS

The TV salesman had stomach muscles like an antique washboard. He was selling a magnificent muscle-building machine of some sort. He said marvelous ABs can be yours in just 30 days. Only $49.95 a month for lotsa months. Next years yard sales will have a lot of them for sale at pennies on the dollar if you want one.

I guess ABs must be abdominal muscles and after my bath that night I took a look at mine. No hard washboard there! I prefer to eat enough so that I don't have wrinkles in my skin. Anyway, I should be getting a new body before long.

God has promised me a new bod and I'm going to take Him at His word. His Word says the new one won't have an ache or pain or blemish. That is the part I like.

Besides reversing the curse from Genesis, our Creator has other surprises for us. There is nothing that defiles in Heaven. Yes, sin and death defile but body waste does too and so our digestive system is in for a redesign. Paul tells us that.

> *For instance, take the matter of eating. God has given us an appetite for food and stomachs to digest it. But that doesn'tmean we should eat more than we need. Don't think of eatingas important, because someday God will do away with bothstomachs and food.*
> *(1 Cor. 6:13)*

#   #   #   #

———END OF THE AGE

For 40 of my 77 years, I have studied end days prophesy. Jesus, His half-brothers and His disciples have all told us what to expect at the end of the age. No, we do not know the hour or day but we are given lots of clues as to the general season. Very few people study the quarter of the Bible that deals with prophesy. Lately, the signs of the end have been coming thick and fast, like a bullet train bearing down on us. It won't be long before I see my Savior, face to face.

I have before me a clipping from my local newspaper. It tells of a Florida company that wants to get a governmental okay to market a tiny computer chip to be embedded under a person's skin to be a permanent ID. Jesus told John about that nearly 2,000 years ago.

> *And he causes all, the small and the great, and the rich and the poor, and the free men and the slaves, to be given a mark on their right hand, or on their forehead, and he provides that no one should be able to buy or to sell, except the one who has the mark. (Rev. 13:16, 17a)*

Don't take the mark!!!!!!!!!!

> *"If anyone worships the beast and his image, and receives a mark on his forehead or upon his hand, he will also drink of the wine of the wrath of God, which is mixed in full strength of His anger; and he will be tormented with fire*

and brimstone in the presence of the holy angels and in the presence o the Lamb."
(Rev. 14:9b,10)

Enough said!

#   #   #   #

———AH, SPRING

How wonderful to see a harbinger of Spring! No, I don't mean a robin, they've been around all winter. It is only February, maybe it's rushing the season, but not according to HT.

"It's the first rummage sale of the season," exclaimed Happy-Toes, "and the Star is taking me." The Star is our youngest daughter and oft-times chauffeur.

One of HT's ministries is the babies of the world. She buys yard sale baby clothes, washes and repairs them as necessary, then she donates them to mission programs. She also gives soap, towels and other necessities to a home for battered women. The mother lode for these things are yard sales. Her favorite things, however, are the baby clothes, which she gives to a home for unwed mothers and to missionaries.

We couldn't afford to buy all these items at new costs, but used prices are generally quite reasonable. Jesus says He approves of her hobby.

> *"When did we see You a stranger and take You in, or naked and clothe You? Or when did we see You sick, or in prison, and come to You? And the King will answer and say to them, Assuredly, I say to you, inasmuch as you did it to one of the least of these My brethren, you did it to Me." (Matt. 25:38-40)*

Do you need a hobby?

#   #   #   #

———GOOD HANDS

"I feel like something that washed up on the beach," said I.

"The EKG shows that your wild heartbeat has gotten even more irregular," said Dr. Mark. "Your heart doesn't pump all the blood you need. You are a candidate for a shock treatment to stabilize your heartbeat."

The procedure involves stopping the heart and then shocking it to start the beat again. Most times it works. I've been trying to get my blood thin enough to suit the doctor by taking rat poison (Warfarin). Now, everything is ready and tomorrow I get electrocuted. I should mention that the good doctor does not care for my terminology.

The long-running TV ad says that you are in good hands with Allstate insurance. I'm in better hands with the Lord's assurance. So, like when I had open-heart surgery, I entrust my heartbeat to God. After all, He started it the first time.

Trust in the Lord with all your heart, and do not lean on your own understanding. In all your ways acknowledge Him, and He will make your paths straight (Prov. 3:5,6)

#   #   #   #

MAURY'S MUSING—HOME

"It had to be 1930 or earlier," said Happy-Toes. "It was before my sister and I went to school."

HT's mother was the organist at Our Savior's Lutheran Church in Bremerton, Washington for 38 years and HT was telling how she first remembered Poulsbo, a small city some 10 miles away, where we now live. Her mother accompanied their pastor Sunday night to play for services at the Children's Home and Happy-Toes and her sister came along.

The Children's Home was a project of local Lutherans. It provided a home for orphan boys as well as keeping those whose parents were in dire straits because of a terrible depression that was in full bloom.

The home was on land farmed by the child residents and provided much of the needed food. Some of the people raised there have great things to say about their time at the home.

That boys home expanded into a large complex and became Martha and Mary, The Home of Loving Kindness. It now has a children's day care, a Christian kindergarten, a seniors apartment house (Ebenezer) and a 170-bed nursing home facility with wings for Alzheimer patients and those needing physical therapy. The old orphan's home is long gone but the nursing home covers the area.

Happy-Toes' mom lived in those Ebenezer Apartments for seven years. She spent the last five days of her life on earth at Martha and Mary Nursing Home. Then, she was transported to Heaven. By my calculations and memory, she left us nearly on the exact same spot where she played the organ at worship seventy years before.

#   #   #   #

———POISON

When our granddaughter Rachael was a baby, and even a little beyond, she ate about anything she could pick up. She swallowed bugs, berries off shrubs and nearly everything else her chubby fingers could grasp. If the local Poison Control Center (PCC) had a poster child, it would have been Rae. I think if the PCC hadn't gotten two calls a week, from Rae's mom, they would have called her to see what was wrong.

Now that Happy-Toes and I are both on blood pressure medication, we fight those pill vial caps. Those caps were put on vials to thwart kids like Rachael. She is now a young lady and it is safe to ask our pharmacist for regular caps instead of those grandma/grandpa proof ones. It's embarrassing to have to ask a grandchild to open our pill bottles.

Just as important as keeping our children from eating something that might be injurious to their physical health is keeping them from swallowing some of the sex and violence that is bad for their mental health. TV and movies are rampant with poison, too. Maybe we should provide child-proof caps for them.

> *Train up a child in the way he should go, even when he is old he will he will not depart from it. (Prov. 22:6)*

# # # #

————HIS PRESENCE

*Come dear Lord, be thou our guest and may
this food to us be blest. (Table prayer.)*

I love this table prayer. For some time I've seen an ad
on TV where a young lady is eating by herself. She has
zapped a Red Baron pizza and as she sits to partake, the
Red Baron himself appears at the table with her.

As I say this prayer with eyes closed, I picture our Lord
appearing next to me.

*And Lo, I am with you always, even to the end
of the age. Matt. 28:20*

# # # #

————AFTER WE'RE GONE

Imagine if you will what life will be like on earth when we Christians, and the Holy Spirit that is within us, are removed from the earth. The decent people from every walk of life——gone! Soldiers and janitors, housewives and statesmen, carpenters and policemen, vanished!

At first, the media will have a field day interviewing pastors and priests who "missed the cut." CNN will feature dozens of people who will say they saw aliens in UFOs kidnap millions of people to populate a colony on Venus.

Then anarchy will take over. And we think "drive-by" shootings are bad now. Murders and rapes and crimes of all types will skyrocket as the devil has his way.

A strong man, the antichrist, will be chosen to bring order out of the chaos. He will bring an evil order that will eclipse the regimes of Hitler, Stalin and Amin. People will still have an opportunity to accept our Lord's grace during this time but if they do, they'll be hunted down and killed. We who have received God's great gift will not be here to witness these evils.

> *For the Lord Himself will descend from heaven with a shout, with the voice of the archangel, and with the trumpet of God; and the dead in Christ shall rise first. Then we who are alive and remain shall be caught up together with them in the clouds to meet the Lord in the air, and thus we shall always be with the Lord.*
> *(1 Thess. 4:16,17)*

\#   \#   \#   \#

———GOOD DEEDS

The man was waiting for his wife to do her Christmas shopping. Sitting in his car, he had read the daily paper. Glancing in his car's side mirror, he saw a meter-maid approach. Thinking of the tired shoppers returning to their autos only to find tickets on their windshields, he went up and down the street dropping his change in expired parking meters. He didn't know the car's owners nor did he expect thanks.

Contrast him with the people in every organization who seek glory and fame from their fellow man. It is nice to get acclaim from others, but the Lord says if that is why we do good deeds, that's all the reward we'll get. Try the secret kind, it's fun!

"Beware of practicing you righteousness before men to be noticed by them; otherwise you have no reward with your Father who is in heaven." (Matt. 6:1)

\#   \#   \#   \#

———ADVICE

Six days each week, at nine a.m., we have a bottle-billiards game at the mobile home park where I reside. It is nearly all the exercise this old cripple gets. My opponents are all pool sharks, though, and I am a pool herring.

Much free advice is offered concerning shot selection. I seem to remember that someone once said that free advice is worth every penny you paid for it. Hilarious laughter follows when someone takes bad advice and fails to connect.

In the game of life, mistakes can have more serious consequences. It is natural to think that when we reach adulthood we are equipped to solve all the problems that come our way. I believe though that we really begin to mature when we seek advice from the wisest source we can find. I use my 66 book library of information from the sages of the ages. The first book is Genesis.

> *All scripture is inspired by God and profitable for teaching, for reproof, for correction, for training in righteousness; that the man of God may be adequate, equipped for every good work. (2 Tim. 3:16,17)*

#   #   #   #

————EXTINCTION

We spend an inordinate amount of time worrying about the future of Snail Darters, Spotted Owls, Flying Lizards and the like when there is nothing we can do about their survival. The world is wearing out! We now have a population in excess of six billion people. Certainly God took this into consideration when He planned an end to this world. We are in the last part of God's day of rest, the seventh day of creation, and He will create again beginning in the millennium. We know He will create then. He said He would change the digestive systems of carnivores and take away the venom from snakes.

Cosmologists have nothing to do with lipstick or eyeliner. They are the scientists who study the universe. They tell us that at least 95% of the plants and creatures that once populated the earth are now extinct. The cosmologists estimate that from two species an hour to five a day die out, never to return.

The scientists say that any species with less that a quadrillion individuals is doomed, eventually. I guess that is why flies, mosquitoes and dandelions are still around.

Even mankind would not survive if it were not for the intervention of a loving Father God and His Son, our Savior. When Jesus comes back to earth with us to rule and reign, peace will return, our God will create again and the whole earth will once again resemble the Garden of Eden!

Also the cow and the bear will graze; their young will lie down together; and the nursing child shall play by the hole of the cobra, and

Maurice (Maury) A. Johnson

the weaned child will put his hand on the viper's den. (Isa. 11:7,8)

\#   \#   \#   \#

———TEMPORARY HOMES

"There's water in my sleeping bag," said Happy-Toes.

"Shut up and go to sleep, it's two a.m.," was my drowsy retort.

Fifteen minutes later, I found I had a water bed, too. This was many years before they were invented! Friends had convinced us that camping was a great way to spend a vacation. They even loaned us their tent. I had my doubts about that 6' by 6' house of waxy cheesecloth. It didn't look like it would keep out mosquitos, let alone rain.

Not being an experienced camper, I hadn't trenched around the tent, nor had I gotten a water-proof tarp to cover the cloth abode. I hadn't even noticed the sign that said Camp Rain Forest when we drove in.

At two-thirty a.m., four very wet, sleepy people and a soggy tent in a Jeep station wagon started the 95 mile drive to a more permanent roof.

God Himself had temporary homes. First, there was the tabernacle. It was God's home while He led the Israelites through the wilderness.

> *Then the cloud covered the tent of meeting, and the glory of the Lord filled the tabernacle. (Exod. 40:34)*

Then there were two temples that were homes for the Lord. The Israelites will complete a third temple during the first half of the seven year Tribulation, but the Antichrist will usurp it for his own glorification. In the coming glorious New Jerusalem, God will not need a home, for He will live with us!

> *And I saw no temple in it, for the Lord God, the*
> *Almighty and the Lamb are it's temple.*
> *(Rev. 21:22)*

#   #   #   #

———PRAYER

I've always been impressed by those who can pray eloquently in front of an audience. I have attended churches where everyone was expected to make long, loud fervent prayers to the Lord. Sometimes, this has made me feel out of place.

In contrast, my prayers are generally silent and come in short sentences. I find it very difficult to pass by a rose or hear a bird sing without thanking God for the great beauty with which He has surrounded us. I must praise Him for the wonderful orderliness of the universe when I see the stars and planets at night. When I think of how God provided for us to know Him, I thank Him for our magnificent salvation.

> *"But you, when you pray, go into your inner room, and when you have shut your door, pray to your Father who is in secret, and your Father who sees in secret will repay you."*
> *(Matt. 6:6)*

I believe God answers all prayers, whether long or short, silent or aloud. I still admire those oral prayers and when we amen them, we assure an answer.

> *"Again I say to you, that if two of you agree on earth about anything that they may ask, it shall be done for them by My father who is in heaven." (Matt. 18:19)*

#   #   #   #

——WHITE AS SNOW

Happy-Toes and I were watching the winter Olympics at Lillehammer, Norway on TV. Glistening snow covered the hills with purity. That snow covering gave me a feeling of peace and serenity.

Later, when we visited the site in person, the snow had melted. No covering concealed the stumps and the brush with beauty.

We are a people who like to remember our guilt even when it is long gone. We look up to God and see all our sins in the way. When God looks down at us, and we are covered with our Savior's blood, we look just like His Son to Him.

> *"Though your sins be as scarlet, they shall be as white as snow; though they are red like crimson, they shall be like wool." (Isa. 1:18b)*

#   #   #   #

————MEMORIES

Each summer for the past few years, a couple of World War 2 bombers have paid a visit to our local airfield. I served as a gunner on the B-17 bomber during the war in Europe. Later, in the Naval Air Reserve I crewed the Navy's version of the B-24. I am drawn like with a magnet to the airstrip. It gives me another chance to take a look at my beloved B-17 and the B-24. Sometimes, when I close my eyes, it gets too real.

One year, the local office of the FAA (Federal Aviation Administration) wouldn't allow one of the planes to fly in our state because it didn't have seatbelts.

My thoughts went back more than 50 years to a wicked war. WE DIDN'T HAVE SEATBELTS. We could have been killed! Come to think of it, I didn't have a seat to put one on.

The fear of man brings a snare, but whoever trusts in the Lord shall be safe. (Prov. 29:25)

\#   \#   \#   \#

Maurice (Maury) A. Johnson

———WHY?

Sometimes it is so hard to accept some of God's truths. Some day, some time if we keep the faith, we will understand why some things happen to us.

They are a lovely Christian couple. He, a college graduate with a fine job. She, a lovely gracious lady. A couple of years after their beautiful church wedding, their dreams were realized when they found out they were expecting.

The couple was elated when they found their firstborn was a beautiful girl. In her first year the doctors discovered that she had a genetic disorder. Despite the prayers of so many, the Lord took her in his arms at the age of one.

Through all the heartbreak and tears, the young mother wrote. She wrote to help others who suffered a similar loss, believing this verse.

> *And we know that God causes all things to work together for good to those who love God, to those who are called according to His purpose. (Romans 8:28)*

I know that I shall see that little girl someday. I know it for the same reason that the kids are welcome to the Lord's table at our congregation each week.

> *But Jesus said, "Let the children alone, and do not hinder them from coming to Me; for the Kingdom of Heaven belongs to such as these." (Matt. 19:14)*

P.S. This couple entered the ministry and are now serving a mid-west congregation.

#   #   #   #

————THREE TIMES

There was a wicked war raging throughout most of the world and many of us made a quick switch from civilian to military life. One of the things I liked least about my changeover was midnight-to-four guard duty. If an intruder violated the boundary of my post, I had specific guidelines to follow.

My instructions were to give three loud warnings of HALT. If the warnings were not heeded, I was to FIRE! Most of the time that would have been difficult because that rifle in my hands was empty or made of wood. I guess I could have hit someone over the head with it though. Three commands really mean something in the military.

Most theologians and denominations cite Matt. 28:19 as the one great commission.

"Go therefore and make disciples of all the nations, baptizing them in the name of the Father and the Son and the Holy Spirit."

I find two great commissions. The second is found in John 21:15-18. Three times our Lord asked Peter, "do you love Me?" When Peter answered in the affirmative, Jesus said, "Tend my lambs," "shepherd my sheep," and "tend my sheep."

Not all of us can be pastors of congregations, but each of us are caretakers of family, friends and neighbors. When a sentry shouts three times, I perk up my ears and when our Lord says something three times, I really sit up and take notice.

#　　#　　#　　#

——————COLD, LUKEWARM

I didn't think I would ever get warm again. It was BR-R-R-R-R cold! The years were 1944 and 1945. I was a gunner on B-17 bombers during World War 2 and all our missions were made at high altitude. The ground temperature in Italy was nice but the outside air at altitude ranged from minus 10 to minus 40 degrees F. Furthermore, the gaps around our gun turrets turned our airplane into a flying wind tunnel. Despite all the clothing I could pile on and still be able to manipulate my gun, I was never even lukewarm.

It appears that it is better to be cold than lukewarm in our Christian walk. In the book of Revelation, the Lord tells John about seven churches in Turkey. These churches represent all churches from the Lord's time until now. They also represent the various denominations and congregations of today.

The city of Laodicea got it's water from hot springs that were some distance from town and by the time water got to town, it was lukewarm. By using this illustration, the Lord made it clear that the Laodicean church lacked spark. The members were well-to-do and had settled into their comfort zone

> *So because you are lukewarm, and neither hot nor cold, I will spit (vomit) you out of my mouth. (Rev. 3:16)*

#   #   #   #

Maurice (Maury) A. Johnson

———DOUBT

Have you ever had times when you doubt the existence of God and His wonderful plan? Boy, I sure have! Sometimes, I think I'm old Satan's favorite doubt target. Those periods of doubt got much shorter as I got older and are practically non-existent now that I'm past the age of 75.

I have only to look out the window to see the flower seeds we planted a couple of months ago up and blooming. A little farther away are the magnificent fir trees that came to being from a tiny seed. My bird houses are full of little chirping creatures and great-grandson Lukey laughs, presto, the Creator is back!

Even Thomas had doubts and he was with the Lord when He did wondrous things. If you are in a wondering mood, look out of the window. You just might see a miracle that came from a seed! We might even have a "leg up" on Thomas.

Jesus said unto him, "Thomas, because you have seen me, you have believed. Blessed are those who have not seen and yet have believed." (John 20:29)

#   #   #   #

———SILENCE

A buddy of mine, figuring he could get an advantage over the deer during hunting season, purchased a used hearing aid at the Salvation Army store. At sunrise on the opening day of season, attired in camouflage, he settled himself comfortably under a huge fir tree with low, sweeping branches. A deer trail was within sight and range. He cranked up the hearing aid volume to full and awaited the footfalls of a trophy buck.

His camo must have worked for a Stellar's Jay landed on the branch above him. The Jay has a loud piercing scream and when he sounded, my friend nearly tore his ear off removing that hearing aid!

I spent some 25 years flying in military aircraft which deafened me. Generally, four 1200 HP noisy engines furnished the accompaniment to my thoughts. Many people I know must have taped music or lectures in their car or even in earphones as they walk or ride.

The world is a very noisy place. I wear hearing aids as a matter of course and often I am thankful for the "off" switch on my aids. It gives me a chance to contemplate God's word without interference and that is when I muse. Do you have a quiet time or place where you can listen to God?

"But the Lord is in His holy temple, let all the earth be silent before Him." (Hab. 2:20)

#   #   #   #

———THE BOTTOM

Happy-Toes set the phone down. "Josh got a steady job," she said.

Grandson Joshua was in high school. He'd delivered newspapers and flyers before, but this was a real job, he said. His job was a dishwasher in a local restaurant, the starting place for many of us. His incentive was the need for gas and insurance for a hoped-for car. It's hardly a glamorous job but the bright side is that there is no place to go but up.

We believers are to rule and reign during our Lord's 1000 year reign on earth. Our position in the millennium will depend on how we handle smaller tasks we have been given during our earthly life.

> *"He who is faithful in what is least is faithful also in much; and he who is unjust in what is least is unjust also in much." (Luke 16:10)*

#   #   #   #

——FEAST

Happy-Toes and I are very dose to our children, their spouses, grandchildren and now our great-grandkids. Our holidays are generally get-togethers where we eat and enjoy each others company.

I had a grand time turning the tables on family and friends when I reached the magical age of three-score-and-ten. I hosted a dinner a party at a local "ribs" restaurant for two dozen family members and friends. Whether salads or ribs dripping with goodness, each had choices of entree. Of course, I had the ribs. Paul, our first great-grandson was a baby and had to get his second hand.

What a celebration and feast we will have in Heaven after the rapture. It's called the Marriage Supper of the Lamb. It's a time when Jesus, and His body, the church will be united FOREVER. I hope at the feast that I will be seated next to Solomon, or John, or Job, or Timothy, or Grandma Johnson, or Noah, or—

> *Then He said to me, "Write: Blessed are those who are called to the marriage supper of the Lamb? And He said to me, "These are the true sayings of God["(Rev. 19:9)*

Picture if you will, tables loaded with the perfect fruits from the Garden of Eden; melting pears, juicy peaches, gorgeous grapes and the finest wine—but no broccoli!

#   #   #   #

157

Maurice (Maury) A. Johnson

———LOSERS

The job was perfect for me! I had prepared a fine resume' and had excellent references. When the list came out, I was the top candidate. The selection was made and it bypassed both me and the person who was second on the list. I don't suppose the reason the third candidate was chosen had anything to do with his being a lodgemate and close friend of the supervisor. I felt like a loser.

You know, Jesus came for us losers! I'll paraphrase what He said in Matthew, chapter five. Blessed are the losers (poor in spirit, mourners, meek) for they shall inherit the

Kingdom of Heaven. Thanks to the Lord, we aren't losers after we accept His pardon!

> *He came to His own, and His own did not receive Him. But as many as received Him, to them He gave the right to become children of God, to those who believe in His name.*
> *(John 1:11,12)*

#　#　#

————SERVICE

The lady of the house pulled on her white gloves and checked the stones around the fireplace for dust and soot while the little girl stood by. Satisfied, the lady removed her gloves. The little Swedish girl was an indentured servant at the age of eight. She was let out to a wealthy family to work as a maid because her family couldn't afford to feed her. Her wage was the equivalent of $25 per year. That little girl was my grandmother.

I was editing a book about Swedish immigrants to this area in the 1870s when I came across this information. These years were bad times economically in the Scandinavian countries. In this country, we strive to "get ahead." We educate ourselves and our children to seek a better line of work. We would like to get rich.

Our Lord didn't put emphasis on doing well, economically. In fact, He told that rich folks sometimes have difficulty obtaining salvation. (Matt.19:23 Luke 1:53) Jesus life on earth emphasized service to all. We believers are told to feed, visit, tend and shepherd our fellow man. He made that clear when He washed the feet of the disciples. I expect that, in heaven, we will continue to serve each other as well as our God.

> *"God resists the proud, but gives grace to the humble." (1 Peter 5:56)*

If we look up over the doors as we leave services at our congregation's building, we can read the carved sign, SERVANT'S ENTRANCE.

# # # #

———FIT

"Drat," I said. At least, I thought I said that. Maybe it was something stronger. The button on the waistband of my trousers had just popped off. I wish they hadn't used rotten thread when they made the pants. Happy-Toes had a suggestion but she couldn't be right because I've worn 36x35s as long as I can remember. Someone else said that our chests slip down some as we get older.

Then, the truth hit me in a flash! Our clothes are mostly made in the Orient now and those people are having trouble converting centimeters to inches. It's no wonder my pants seem to be smaller. I'm getting larger trousers now to make up the manufacturer's lack of math skills. Besides, there could be some shrinkage. Well, I know there is one place I fit.

> *So then you are no longer strangers and aliens but you are fellow citizens with the saints, and are of God's household, having been built upon the foundation of the apostles and prophets, Christ Jesus Himself being the cornerstone, in whom the whole building, being fitted together is growing into a holy temple in the Lord; in whom you also are being built together into a dwelling of God in the Spirit. (Eph. 2:19-22)*

#   #   #   #

————THE KING IS COMING

We knew a few months in advance about the planned visit of King Harald and Queen Sonya to our small Norwegian theme hamlet. We had ample time to paint and clean before the visit of the Norwegian royal couple. The town was spotless and a great celebration was planned. The entire royal visit lasted three hours.

We have ample notification that greater royalty is coming. He is the King of Kings! From my forty years study of Bible prophesy, I am convinced that it could be before I finish writing this piece. At most, it must be within a very few years.

Unlike King Harald's visit with us, we will go to visit with our King and live in His town forever. Meanwhile, I'll try to clean up my mind and habits to be more presentable to Him.

> *"In My Father's house are many dwelling places; If it were not so, I would have told you; for I go to prepare a place for you."*
> *(John 14:2)*

\#   \#   \#   \#

Maurice (Maury) A. Johnson

————REUNIONS

I enjoy my high school reunions. As someone put it, high school was the best seven years of my life. It's fun to see my classmates, now older with bald heads and paunches, and the guys are in even worse shape. Just kidding! I was honored to be asked to deliver the prayer at my 52nd. It went—.

Dear Father in Heaven. We thank You for this glorious day that You have given us. A day when we share wonderful memories with friends and classmates we love. Friends with whom we have shared a tender part of our lives and who have shared theirs with us—forever friends.

Now as we hear each other through hearing aids, see each other through seeing aids and converse through dental aids, let us relive the joys of our youth. We remember those who are no longer with us. We ask Your blessings for those who are not with us because of illness or infirmity.

We ask Your blessings on all present as we are transported back to a joyous, carefree time. We ask You to bless this food to our bodies in Jesus' name and for His sake. Amen.

#   #   #   #

————THISTLES AND MUSTARD

When I had very small feet (it was a very long time ago), it was one of my jobs to pull the mustard plants out of our hayfield while disturbing the hay as little as possible. Dad believed that the taste of our milk was affected by that pesky weed. It was quite a chore for a little guy who would rather be climbing trees.

A few years ago when we were in Scandinavia, we saw whole fields of mustard that were evidently planted on purpose. I got to wondering if some small child had to go through those fields and weed the hay out.

Anyway, this proves that a weed is just a plant that grows where we don't want it. We didn't have any weeds until Adam and Eve sinned.

Cursed is the ground because of you; in toil you shall eat of it all the days Of your life, both thorns and thistles it shall grow for you. (Gen. 3:17b: 18a)

Roses, thistles and blackberries didn't have thorns, either. Without weeds, during the millenium, farming will be a pleasure for those who are still in their earthly bodies.

And there shall no longer be any curse; (Rev. 22:3a)

Little kids will be able to climb trees to their heart's content.

#   #   #   #

———DECISION

Once upon a time I had a boss who was very indecisive. We, in the engineering office, wasted a lot of time awaiting a yes or no from him. We threatened to call his wife and tell her not to cut his lunchtime sandwich in two lest he go hungry trying to decide which half to eat first.

Many people have a tough time making a decision to serve God. If we don't accept Jesus' ransom for our sins, we are automatically serving the only alternative. That is death.

Some people think they'll make a choice for Christ on their deathbed. Often there is an accident, heart attack or stroke and—presto, no deathbed.

I've never regretted my decision. It's been a great source of joy to me.

> *For the wages of sin is death but the free gift of God Is eternal life in Christ Jesus our Lord (Rom. 6:23)*

# # # #

———TREES

I heard on the radio that a environmentalist lady had sponsored a funeral for a—tree! She had hired a minister and planned for 100 mourners.

Just as in St. Paul's day, many seem hell-bent (the right words) to worship the created rather than the Creator. I wonder who will furnish the funerals for one-third of the world's trees that will burn up during the coming Tribulation period. (Rev.8:7)

That coffin must have been a dandy. I wonder what it was made of?

> *For they exchanged the truth of God for a lie,*
> *and worshiped and served the creature rather*
> *than the Creator, who is blessed forever.*
> *Amen Romans 1:25*

#   #   #   #

Maurice (Maury) A. Johnson

————CHANGE

I turned off the ignition and reached for the brown bag beside me. I slipped the bag with the cut-out eye holes over my head and entered the front of the building. I thrust my head in the door, looked both ways, and removed the bag.

Ramona looked askance. I explained that this was the first time I had come to a beauty shop for a haircut and I wanted to make sure none of my pool playing buddies would see me enter a place called Fluff and Stuff.

Happy-Toes had complained about my "Old Geezer" haircut. I don't know where she got that idea. It's the same kind of haircut I've had since 1945 and she hadn't complained before. Anyway, HT and her beauty operator had conspired and made an appointment for me.

Things sure change. I am now acquainted with mousse, blow dry and the layered look. It is nice to know that some things never change.

Jesus Christ is the same yesterday and today, yes and forever. (Heb. 13:8)

\#   \#   \#   \#

166

———JALAPENOS

There is something great about watching baseball played on green grass in the sunshine in the middle of winter. After about two weeks of steady wind up North, I was ready to sample the good life.

Our local major league ball team has a training complex in Arizona and plays a schedule of pre-season games lasting about a month. For several years, I would enjoy a week or two of relaxation under the sun at the ballpark.

I had purchased my hotdog and was piling on the goodies; four scoops of jalapenos, three of onions and lots of mustard. A lady with a wrinkled nose was looking over my shoulder at the condiment bar.

"Is that good," she asked.

I told her, they are if you get them before the fourth inning, After that, they tend to shrivel. I realized later that she might have been referring to the goodies atop the wiener.

I love peppers and I think the Lord does, too. We Christians are the salt that adds flavor to life and I believe some of us are the peppers that add fire! Take Elijah or John the Baptist for instance. Viva the Jalapenos!

Let your speech always be with grace, seasoned, as it were, with salt, so that you may know how You should respond to each person. (Col 4:6)

\#   \#   \#   \#

————THIS IS THE DAY

This is the day that Hard-Hearted Hannah has awaited for 17 years. Let me hasten to explain that Happy-Toes' sister is far from hard-hearted. She received that nickname many years ago from her son, then a teenager. It was when the song by that name was popular.

Back to "the day." Hannah and her husband have spent the last 17 winters in the sunny Phoenix area with their two children and their families. This year they are staying up North.

Hannah has missed SNOW! Last night it snowed about two inches. It was wet, but it was snow and it made Hannah happy.

This is the day which the Lord has made; Let us rejoice and be glad in it. (Psa. 118:24)

\#   \#   \#   \#

────BROKEN NOSES

"Aw, c'mon, they can't all have broken noses, not with those face guards!"

I was referring to the football players sitting on the bench during an NFL game. Many of them had a strip of tape across the bridge of their nose. I thought they must be decorations like the ear-rings. In my day, with leather helmets sans face guards, busted proboscises were common.

Sometime later, we saw a TV show where the entire studio audience was wearing the same kind of nose strip. The MC explained that he and his wife had cured their snoring problems by wearing those things to bed.

Happy-Toes disappeared in the direction of the nearest drug store. When she reappeared, she presented me with a box of Breathe Rights.

As a result of breaking my schnoz several times, I have a restricted air flow. Using those adhesive strips seemed to double my air supply. They worked!

I wonder if Happy-Toes sleeps sound enough so I can stick one on her?

Praise Him with timbrel and dancing; Praise Him with stringed instruments and pipe Praise Him with loud cymbals; Praise Him with resounding cymbals. Let everything that has breath praise the Lord Praise the Lord! (Psa. 150:3,4,5,)

\# \# \# \#

169

Maurice (Maury) A. Johnson

———CELEBRATIONS

Happy-Toes just celebrated another birthday. She and her lady friends milk a birthday for all it is worth! They seem to think that each one must be feted with six luncheons, three restaurant dinners and a picnic or two.

On the other hand, we men generally forget ours until the policeman tells us that our driver's license has expired. One of my sons-in-law recently forgot his TWIN sister's birthday and even her age.

The Hebrews have many celebrations or feasts. Each one commemorates God's great goodness to the Jews and each one reminds us of an event in the life of Jesus. We celebrate one of those feasts in our congregation. It is the Seder Meal, enjoyed at Passover and it reminds us of the blood covering for our sins that our Savior provided.

> *Whom God displayed publicly as a propitiation in His blood through faith. This was to demonstrate His righteousness, because in the forbearance Of God He passed over the sins previously committed (Romans 3:25)*

#   #   #   #

———SIMPLE LIFE

It was the first day of the month and as I flipped the calendar page, I was greeted with penciled notations on the first two weeks worth of squares. Happy-Toes is very faithful to note our appointments. Sometimes, we forget to look at the calendar, though. I looked at those busy notes and my mind harkened back to a simpler time.

Knute was typical of a half-dozen bachelors who lived in the great forested lands around our small farm. His needs were few and he made a meager existence by selling firewood and a few logs. From time to time, my dad or my uncles would check on these men to see if they were OK.

I was a wee lad as the Model T jolted over the rough road to the small clearing. The cleared patch contained a tiny crude cabin, an outhouse and many fir stumps. An axe was stuck in a chopping block near the door and smoke curled from the tin stack.

Knute opened the cabin door as the Ford chugged to a stop and he beckoned us in. The old Scandinavian kicked the top off a bracken fern that was growing through a knot-hole in the shiplap floor and reached for a blackened coffee pot. He enjoyed the company and wiped out two stained cups with a rag that was equally stained.

As the adults conversed, I looked around the cabin. There was a home-made bed with feather tick, a small table with two chairs and a wood stove. From nails in the wall, hung a fry pan and a battered hat. It was a simple life.

We can't always simplify our lives as much as Knute did, but we can make a difference in the way we live. Maybe by simplifying we can find more time to study

171

God's Word and talk to Him and not so much time dusting nick-nacks.

> *For our boasting is this; the testimony of our conscience that we conducted ourselves in the world in simplicity and Godly sincerity, not with fleshly wisdom but by the grace of God, and more abundantly toward you.*
> *(2 Cor. 1:12)*

#   #   #   #

———MUSIC MAN

I happened to turn on the TV and catch Andre' Rieu and his wonderful Viennese Orchestra playing a Strauss waltz. Then it was the Beautiful Blue Danube and even a Glen Miller medley. My heart soared.

I love to listen to beautiful music, but making it is another matter. When I was but a wee lad, my mother decided that I should take piano lessons. She had a piano and she loved it although she had mastered only the most rudimentary basics of that ivory-keyed instrument. I failed to catch on to those basics.

A year or so later, my dad decreed that I must take up the violin. He had a fiddle and would pick it up at times to "chord." He was born with crippled fingers but he loved the music those strings would produce. Again, I didn't pass, I still didn't understand the basics of music.

I really should have been a singer. When I was young, we didn't have automatic toasters. The units had drop-down sides and you had to remember to check the toast often lest it would burn.

"It's good for your voice," said mom as she scraped the blackened bread in the sink. From the amount of charcoal I ate, I should star in grand opera!

Well, neither the piano nor the fiddle lessons took and my voice still sounds like Froggy the Gremlin. I flunked those lessons but I could have failed in anything musical. I do sing in church (not good, but I sing loud to make up for it).

When we pause to think about it, music is one of the many perfect creations of our wonderful God. Just eight musical notes, with their sharps and flats, yet an infinite variety of combinations to please us and glorify Him. When I get to Heaven, I won't need a basket to carry a tune in. Then, I'll be able to sing His praises, both loud and good!

> *Sing aloud to God our strength; Make a joyful shout to the God of Jacob, Raise a song and strike the timbrel, The pleasant harp with the lute (Psa. 81:1)*

#   #   #   #

——————THEOLOGIANS

Happy Toes admits to not being a great scholar. In fact, she was afraid she would not get her high school diploma. During her junior and senior years of high school, World War 2 was being waged and she also worked eight hours a day. During that era all our efforts went toward winning the war so book knowledge took a back seat to that.

I am a member of a computer listserv that emphasizes problems in theology. Most of the members are pastors and seminary professors or students. Often, the search for an answer is merely an exercise in futility. The Lord chooses not to give us all the answers, now, but in the future when we have more of the mind of God we will understand. Until then, we are to accept His truths by faith. Faith is the key! It is the reason that children and illiterates can achieve greater heavenly rewards than seminary professors.

We tend to over-analyze and over-complicate everything. Rustics like Billy Sunday and D. L. Moody accepted biblical truths they didn't understand and they won thousands to the Lord. An old hymn writer put it this way.

Trust and obey For there's no other way, To be happy in Jesus Than to trust and obey.

#   #   #   #

175

———RECYCLING

When my homesteading grandfather hewed his farm from the forest, one of his necessary buildings was a workshop. That shop building was divided into sections according to use. I remember a carpenter shop and a blacksmith shop. As a 5-or-6-year-old in 1929, I don't remember much about the wood shop, but the smithy shop stands out in my mind. The forge in the center of the room was hot. I attempted to work the bellows for grandpa but I was too short on one end. Grandpa laughed at my feeble efforts and took over that chore himself.

Nothing made of iron or steel was ever wasted. The precious metal was recycled and returned to service in another form. It became tools or hardware or some other needed item. When my parents were married, Dad's uncle gave him a precious gift. It was a pitchfork.

Are you ready to be recycled? As a Christian, I am. If you are a believer, you are, too. When the Lord calls us at the rapture, we'll get new bodies. Bodies that can be recognized from our worldly ones, but very different. These new ones won't even have a wart, pimple, wrinkle or in-grown toenail.

Our characters will be similar, though, to what we have here. These are worth, developing down here on earth. Are we generous, friendly and loving? Other parts of us will go through God's brain and heart wash. We will be sanctified. My Webster's tells me that means to be purified or freed from sin or to be made holy.

Now may the God of peace Himself sanctify you entirely; and may your spirit and soul and body be preserved complete, without blame at the coming of our Lord Jesus Christ.
(1 Thess. 5:23)

#   #   #   #

Maurice (Maury) A. Johnson

———CHURCH SPEAK

Over the years, I have been pleased to have friends visit our home congregation. Many times that visit was their first and last. Having been raised in the church, I really didn't understand. I did get word that some folks felt our congregation was too high-class for them, Some of these people later joined churches of other denominations. Now, I think I know one of the reasons why.

Jargon is a language that is peculiar to group of people. It may apply to a certain trade, vocation, field of science or even, unfortunately, theology. It is a language that is a form of shorthand for those who are "in the know" to communicate with each other. Unfortunately, church-speak often becomes a barrier when pastors or priests use it while preaching to those who are not churched,

When the Lord led us to a different town, we found the 56 mile round trip to our former congregation was a bit much at our age. We asked God for direction and began visiting nearby congregations. When we attended a local group just beginning to worship together, we knew this is it.

We have mod music with lots of amplifiers, plays or video clips, great sermons and wonderful prayers for community and personal needs. We appeal to the young, unchurched families. We are growing fast, and, oh, you won't find any church-speak there.

#   #   #   #

178

————THE TWO FACES OF JOHN

The normally mild-mannered baseball manager really blew his stack. The game was a close one and the blown call by the umpire could well affect the game. The manager ranted and raved, then kicked dirt on the umpire. He pulled up a base and threw it as far as he could. Oft-times, a sharp coach will put on a display like this to enliven his team. In this case, it did for the team made a comeback and won. That ploy loosened up the players.

Our God has an angry side, too, and of all the characters in the Bible, John knew the faces of God best. John was often referred to as "the disciple whom Jesus loved." In his gospel, he reflected that love in a mighty way.

Our Lord also entrusted him with knowledge of His anger as told in the book of Revelation. Here, God's anger falls upon those who won't accept His amnesty of love. Even in His anger, He gives all a last chance.

Perfect book-ends to His Word; first, His love for us through creation. (Genesis) Then, when we couldn't handle it and gave it away to Satan, He rescues us. In Revelation, God gives Satan his comeuppance. Then, it's back to love again.

Much more then, having now been justified by His blood, we shall be saved from the wrath of God through Him. (Rom. 5:9)

\#   \#   \#   \#

————LANGUAGES

"I'm sorry, lady, I don't understand you, maybe my wife can." I handed the phone to Happy-Toes.

After trying to make sense of what the lady on the other end of the wire was saying, HT gave up, also. We get an awful lot of calls from tele-marketeers and from some of our favorite ministries where the person who is calling evidently has English as a second language.

At one time, regional accents and languages just here in the USA were quite different. In the late 1930s and early 40s, radio stations were choosing up sides and becoming networks. Because of more pure English and less dialect difference, most network radio announcers were drawn from the Pacific Northwest. It was my ambition to be one until a great big war came along and changed everything.

Once upon a time the whole world spoke the same language until God decided that was not to be. After the flood, he told everyone to spread out and fill the earth but they clung together and built a city. He confused their languages so they obeyed. We will have one language when the Lord comes back!

> *On that day I will purify the lips of all people, so that everyone will be able to worship the Lord together. (Zeph. 3:9)*

#   #   #   #

————MODEL T

The picture of the Model T Ford brought a rush of memories. I had gotten a catalogue of miniature autos in the mail. The model cars appeared to be exact replicas of the real thing.

It was about 1928. There was no heater in our "'Tin Lizzie," and the fabric and isinglass or mica curtains did little to hold out the cold. It got worse. In 1929, when my brother was born, my seat was moved to the tiny pick-up box in the real cold. The cab on that flivver was small and there was no room for a 5-year-old boy, Dad, Mama and baby, too.

We seldom went visiting in the evening. We did go to special church services and to visit my grandparents home some five miles away. During the fall and winter visits, I would normally fall asleep and have to be awakened for the cold trip home.

A lot of things have changed in the field of transportation in the last seven decades. Now, warm cars, paved roads and air conditioning have made personal transportation a breeze. We don't have to jack up the car's drive wheel and crank the engine to life either.

There is one thing that hasn't changed and I'm very thankful for that. Our God is so far ahead of us that He doesn't have to correct anything. Some heretics try to change our Savior God, though.

Jesus Christ is the same yesterday, today, and forever. So do not be attracted by strange, new ideas. (Heb. 13:8, 9a)

#   #   #   #

Maurice (Maury) A. Johnson

———VOICE

The steel walls of the great airplane hangar seemed to resonate with the sound of many aircraft engines. Four of our Navy patrol planes were being checked out for the days flights on the tarmac just outside the hangar. As I was the Leading Chief, it was my duty to muster 142 men and Chief Petty Officers inside.

At this "start-of-the-day" meeting, I took roll and passed on the information necessary to carry out the activities of the day. It was part of my job to see that all the troops understood these orders. My voice carries well and it probably was part of the reason I got the job.

I close my eyes and imagine our Lord on the shores of the Sea of Galilee teaching the multitudes. He didn't have a public address system either, but, He taught 5,000 men, not counting the women and children. Every pastor will tell you that you can't get 25 people together without folks coughing and babies crying causing background noise. To be heard by so many in this situation was a major accomplishment. On another occasion, we are told He had an audience of 4,000 men plus women and kids. His voice must have made mine sound like a whisper. It must have been very pleasant with all the love He has for us all. God, the Father has a very commanding voice. It is compared to "seven thunders;" and "many waters."

There will come a time, however, when the voice of Jesus will not be so pleasant. At the end of the millennium He will be the judge that sends the unbelievers to the Lake of fire.

His feet were as bright as bronze refined in a furnace, and His voice thundered like mighty ocean waves. (Rev. 1:15)

#   #   #   #

Maurice (Maury) A. Johnson

————PAINS AND THORNS

"It's a good thing a marijuana salesman didn't knock on my door at 6 a.m. this morning," I told the doctor, "I would have been sorely tempted." "It took me 15 minutes to get out of bed." "Although, I've spent much of my life with pain, I-know now what excruciating pain is."

Election day is coming close and each time an attempt to legalize that substance is on the ballot. It's claimed that smoking the leaf will alleviate the problem for those who have chronic pain.

"Don't call that "grass" salesman, Maury," said the doctor as she handed me a batch of pain pill samples. "You are loaded with arthritis." I am told that everyone who is over 40 has a start of that problem. I've had nearly twice that many years to grow mine.

Despite my prayers to have the Lord to rid me of that problem, He hasn't seen fit to do so. Maybe Paul had arthritis, too. He wrote about his "thorn in the flesh."

I don't want anyone to think more highly of me than what they can actually see in my life and my message, even though I have received wonderful revelations from God. But to keep me from getting puffed up, I was given a thorn in my flesh, a messenger from Satan to torment me and keep me from getting proud. Three different times I begged the Lord to take it-away. Each time He said, "My gracious favor is all you need.

184

My power works best in your weakness."
(2-Cor. 12:6b-9a)

\#   \#   \#   \#

————GOOD NEWS

We are so used to seeing bad news on TV newscasts or in the day's paper. It's great to see some good stuff once in a while. To those of us who study end-days prophesy, our newspaper brings a good news/bad news mix. Jesus tells us that some of this bad stuff is going to happen before we believers go home to Heaven. Matthew, chapter 24, lists bad things, some of which we can expect in these, the end days.

But, there is also some good news. A few years ago, The Lausanne Task Force on the progress of evangelism compiled these numbers. They tell of the growth of Christianity worldwide.

In 1430, there was one Christian in 99 of the world's population.

In 1790, there was one Christian in 49 of the world's population.

In 1940, it was one in 32 and 1970, one in 19. One in 13 in 1983.

In 1994, one in 10 were Christians.

The Christian Broadcasting Network and Trinity Broadcasting Network spread the Good News via satellite TV to hundreds of millions. If your congregation is on the ball, you no doubt support mission and evangelistic efforts, too.

"And the Good News about the Kingdom will be preached throughout the whole world; so that all nations will hear it; and then, finally, the end will come." (Matt. 24:14)

The whole world won't be reached with the Gospel until after we are gone via the Rapture. The 144,000 Jewish Billy Grahams will finish the job during the tribulation. (*Rev. chap. 7)*

#   #   #   #

———WORSHIP

A bigger than life size statue of Jesus with arms outstretched caught my eye as we stepped through the double doors. The stained glass windows and the polished wood of the altar and communion rail were a familiar sight and we found seats on a gleaming wood pew near the pipe organ and choir loft. This was the church of Happy-Toes youth and the place where we were married. We worshiped here for the first ten years of our marriage. From time to time we come back to bid goodbye to old friends or to celebrate wedding anniversaries.

Contrast that scene to this. We step into the high school multi-purpose room. Many banners of mottos from classes past greet us from the overhead. Handshakes and hugs are in order and we smell the coffee.

Some take their coffee and doughnuts to round school tables. Happy-Toes and I make our way to chairs down front in what we like to call deaf row. More handshakes and greetings await us there. The solid Word is preached in a less formal setting, but our Lord is in this place, too.

Our Lord will happily accept our worship whether we prefer to worship in a casual or formal setting. The only necessary thing is to have our heart in it!

> *"For where two or three gather together because. they are mine, I am there among them." (Matt. 18:20)*

# # # #

———GRIEF

I greeted the group of high school students that were gathered around the flagpole.

They were making a memorial of flowers and signs to the memory of a fellow student who had committed suicide the day before. It was Sunday morning and Happy-Toes and I were headed for our worship service in the high school commons.

Some of the students followed us in. At the end of the service, pastor called on the students who came forward and they told of their friendship with the departed sophomore and of their grief. We grieved with them. The message had been one of a series on prayer and it is our custom to pray for congregational needs. Now pastor's prayer was one of solace.

A situation like this must really tear at the heart or-pastors and those that console. How can parents and friends cope when a child's life is ended at such a young age? We can only trust in our eternal God for consolation. I believe that when we mourn, our Lord mourns with us.

> *"God blesses those who mourn, for they shall be comforted." (Matt. 5:4)*

#

> *Rejoice with those who rejoice, and weep with those who weep. (Rom. 12:15)*

#   #   #   #

Maurice (Maury) A. Johnson

———THE WAY TO PRAY

Sometimes, denominational differences can be rather small. I found this poem that explains the proper way to pray, so I'll have to start a new denomination. I'll have to call it the Headstand Church.

The proper way for a man to pray,
Says Deacon Lemuel Keys,
And the only proper attitude
is down upon his knees.

No, I should say the way to pray,
Says Reverend Doctor Wise
Is standing straight with outstretched arms
and rapt and upturned eyes.

Oh no, no, no said Elmer Slow,
Such posture is too proud,
A man should pray with eyes fast closed
And head contritely bowed.

It seems to me that hands should be
Austerely clasped in front,
Both hands pointing at the ground,
Said Reverend Doctor Blunt.

Last year, I fell in Hutchkins' well,
Head first, said Cyrus Brown,
And both my heels were stickin' up,
And my head was pointing down.

And I made a prayer right then and there,
The best prayer I ever said.
The prayinest prayer I ever prayed,
Was standin' on my head.

Sam Walter Foss

Maurice (Maury) A. Johnson

———THE FAMILY

I'm the kind that wakes up all fuzzy every morning wondering who I am or where I am. Happy-Toes hates it when I get up first. When I do, she has a real kitchen clean-up job to do. I spill. You see, l have to prime my heart with two mugs of coffee before it'll pump.

This morning I awoke bright-eyed and bushy-tailed. No cobwebs and the coffee was brewing on the counter without tile usual-attendant mess. It was about two hours before sun-up and I was sitting in my chair. My Bible was by my side unopened, and the lamp was unlit.

A still, small voice spoke to my mind. It said FAMILY. It was not aloud, but-it, seemed to penetrate every atom in me. With the word came a great understanding of the importance of the family to God. I believe one of the highest callings God-can give is to shepherd a family! Not all are selected for this honor. Even the Lord's disciples were not all accorded this privilege.

What are the duties of a shepherd? A shepherd attends his/her flock, keeps them fed, sheltered, out of trouble and leads them. Sometimes, it's necessary to administer loving discipline. A shepherd encourages, is generous with love, and teaches all about our wonderful God and Savior.

> *Like a shepherd He will tend His flock in His arms He will gather the lambs, and carry them in His bosom; He will gently lead the nursing ewes. (Isa. 40:11)*

#　#　#　#

192

————HEART MUSIC

With a song in my heart, and a—and I can't remember the next line. That is the start of a song of yesteryear.

With me, that is not only a song, it's also a truism. I often find myself singing inside. That is good because my singing outside is not that great. My inner rich baritone turns into Mr. Froggy Voice by the time it escapes my lips.

Oh, I do have excuses. My asbestosis and my congestive heart failure and then there is the heart operation when they had that garden hose down my throat for eight hours,

Maybe it's the high altitude flying or the—. I think I'll skip the excuses and just enjoy the inner songs.

The refrains of *The Old Rugged Cross* and *How Great Thou Art* stick with me for days after we sing them in church. The strains of *Danny Boy* or *The Green, Green Grass of Home* haunt me for a long while after I have heard them. *El'Paso, Wolverton Mountain* and any *Sousa March* wind me up also. I figure I'll really be able to sing when I get to Heaven because the Lord won't want my sour notes there.

I will sing to the Lord as long as I live. I will praise my God to my last breath! (Psa. 104:33)

#   #   #   #

Maurice (Maury) A. Johnson

————PEANUTS

There is something about peanuts in the shell. Even the smell takes me to the ballpark and sometimes to Walter's living room. Many older people I've known enjoy the nation's pastime and Happy-Toes' grandfather was always totally absorbed in the radio account of the home team's baseball games. Walter was a butcher and most butchers of his day were missing a finger or two. Walter had a very short right thumb and used it to crack the nut shells. I thought of Walter and smiled as I dropped a handful of goobers in my bird feeder.

I've never seen a Stellar's Jay eat a peanut, I have placed many pounds of the nuts in my bird feeders over the years and I've watched as the Jays carried them away. I have dug up a lot of those goobers when I've been weeding. God in His infinite wisdom gave birds an instinct to plant seeds to propagate plants for our food and pleasure.

Those peanuts were like the Word of God in Jesus' story of the farmer planting seed. He first tells the story and then explains it's meaning.

> *"This is the meaning of the story. The seed is God's message. The seed that fell on the hard path represents those who hear the message, but then the Devil comes and steals it away and prevents them from believing and being saved. The rocky soil represents those who hear the message with joy, but like young plants in such soil, their roots don't go very deep. They believe for a while, but they wilt*

when the hot winds of testing blow. The thorny ground represents those who hear and accept the message, but all too quickly the message is crowded out by the cares and riches and pleasures of this life. And so they never grow into maturity. But the good-soil represents honest, good-hearted people who hear God's message, cling to it, and steadily produce a huge harvest. (Luke 8:11-15')

\#   \#   \#   \#

Maurice (Maury) A. Johnson

———UNCLE

"Tell Mom and Dad that I'll' be there ere too long, Uncle," I thought.

The occasion was my 97-year-old uncle's memorial service. Several rows of the beautiful Baptist Church where he had attended were filled with his family and friends. He had three children, 12 grandchildren and 20 great-grandchildren.

The picture displayed among the flowers showed him in a very familiar pose. Uncle was wearing his wonderful smile and his battered fishing hat. I smiled back. Uncle Fred was in Heaven.

The familiar hymns are never tiring at a Christian's funeral; How Great Thou Art, It is Well With My Soul, Precious Lord and Because He Lives take on new fresh meaning at a time like this. The 23rd Psalm was as fresh as the beautiful flowers at the chancel.

As friend after friend rose to tell of this gentle man, a young boy took the microphone. He was the son of Uncle's housekeeper.

"He taught me about Jesus and he brought me to church," he said. Only then, did tears flow.

For years Uncle had' cared for Auntie through-the stages of Alzheimer's Yet, he found time to visit my ailing parents regularly. My late brother and I referred to him as Saint Frederick. He truly is, you know.

And may the Lord make you increase and abound in love to one another and to all, just as we do to you, so that He may establish your hearts blameless in holiness before our God and Father at the coming of our Lord Jesus Christ with all His saints. (1Thess. 3:13)

\#   \#   \#   \#

————SIXTY?

"Do you think we'll ever make sixty, asked Happy-Toes.

"I dunno, all the signs say that the Lord is coming soon to take us out of here."

The occasion was our 58th wedding anniversary. HT and I have hit it off pretty well for more than half a century. We attribute much of that to three generations of praying families.

It was December 7, 1941. Events of that day turned our world upside down. I was a senior in high school and too young to join the service. After graduation, while awaiting my 18th birthday to join, I went to work in the local Navy shipyard to aid the war effort.

Happy-Toes was a year behind me in school: God formed-her just nine months after I was born. I believe He did it just for me. For her part of the war effort, she went to classes for four hours and worked for eight. There in a navy facility, love bloomed.

I got home for just five days from the Army Air Corps when we got married, each of us were 19 years old; Then, it was off to fight the air war in Europe. We grew up fast, then.

In the days of Mary and Joseph, the marrying age was different. The groom was probably 20 or 21. He had been educated by his father or a teacher in the synagogue. He then served an apprenticeship in his chosen trade before marrying. The bride would be about 12 or 13, maybe 14. She'd be schooled-by her mother in cooking and sewing and possibly reading.

Give honor to marriage, and remain faithful to one another in marriage God will surely judge people who are immoral and those who commit adultery. (Heb. 13: 4)

#   #   #   #

———EUNUCHS

"Why don't they just make eunuchs out of them," said my friend.

We had been discussing the terrible rash of child kidnappers and murderers filling the news. How could we halt the serial sex crimes? Would castration be a deterrent? At least, it should cut down the amount of future victims.

"Believe me," he said, "They'd lose all sexual desires." My friend had lost body parts as the result of a cancer operation.

Maybe it wouldn't be such a bad idea after all. Once upon a time it was common practice to castrate servants and captives who worked around palaces and harems. The bright young men captured in the Babylonian invasion off Jerusalem fit that category. Daniel, Ezekiel, Shadrach, Meshach and Abednego were in that group. These young men were under the control of the master of the eunuchs. (Dan. 1:3) The prophet Isaiah had foretold the exile some 150 years earlier.

> *Nothing will be left, says the Lord. Some of your own descendants will be taken away into exile. They will become eunuchs in the palace of Babylon's king. (Isa. 6b, 7)*

Evidently, being a eunuch does not affect mental capacity adversely because Daniel rose to a very high position in the Babylonian Empire.

#   #   #   #

———DUTY

We had a neighbor lady who was very active in community affairs. She was a leader in the League of Women Voters, had several offices in her church congregation, the Garden Club and led a great many causes. Many looked up to her as a leader, but not her three children. She didn't have much time for them.

The kids grew up like Topsy and mostly fended for themselves. Consequently, they didn't "turn out well."

Is our first duty to our family or our community? I believe our time can be better spent if we tend to first things first. I think many things we think are necessary are just a copout.

Children are a gift from God and if He gives us kids, we'd better take care of them.

> *These older women must train the younger women to live quietly, to love their husbands and their children, and to be sensible and clean minded, spending their time in their own homes, being kind and obedient to their husbands, so that the Christian faith can't be spoken against by those who know them.*
> *(Titus 2:4,5)*

#   #   #   #

Maurice (Maury) A. Johnson

———MUSHROOMS

I have never been much on mushrooms. In fact, one of my mottos has been, "Let there be no fungus among us." When I find them on a restaurant salad, I generally relocate them to Happy-Toes' plate. I do tolerate them in gravy served on meat, though.

During our trip to Finland, we were served a most delicious soup with our dinner. You guessed it, it was mushroom soup!

God said everything He made was good—except broccoli of course!

And God saw all that He had made, and behold, it was very good. And there was and there was evening and there was morning, the sixth day. (Gen. 1:31)

#　　#　　#　　#

─────BEAUTY

"Beauty comes from within," an old saying goes. Happy-Toes and I have an old friend who we both think is a beautiful lady. She is most gracious and wears the nicest smile. We have known her for more than 55 years. Both of us score her a perfect ten.

An acquaintance was talking about our friend one day and mentioned that her nose and ears were too big. That person evidently never heard the great maxim, "you can't raise yourself up by tearing someone else down."

Here is how to score beauty on the **Acme Little Daisy Maurymeter**. A perfect score is ten.

> *Loves people*---------------------- *plus 2*
> *Smiles a lot* ----------------------- *plus 2*
> *Has sense of humor*-------------- *plus 2*
> *Encourages others*--------------- *plus 2*
> *Is generous* ---------------------- *plus 2*

But wait! There is more.

> *Is self-centered* ------------------- *minus 2*
> *Talks about others* --------------- *minus 2*
> *Hates somebody*------------------ *minus 2*
> *No sense of humor* --------------- *minus 2*
> *Is selfish*-------------------------- *minus 2*

Don't be concerned about the outward beauty that depends on jewelry, or beautiful clothes, or hair arrangement. Be beautiful inside, in

> *your hearts, with the lasting charm of a gentle*
> *and quiet spirit which is so precious to God.*
> *(1 Peter 3:3,4)*

You are welcome to use the Maurymeter.

#   #   #   #

————MISSIONS

The man reached into a secret place and withdrew a tape recorder. He pushed the play button and the voice began. "Your mission, should you to choose to accept it is—." Thus began a television program of yesteryear, Mission Impossible. Our walk with the Lord begins with the phrase, mission possible. As we submit ourselves to God's will, He makes known His missions for us. No, not all of us will be sent to deepest, darkest Africa as missionaries. Just as our body parts have different uses, we, the parts of our Lords body, have different functions.

I know about some of my missions. One of them is putting my musings on paper. Hopefully these writings will make someone's walk with the Lord more joyful. Do you know what your missions are?

For just as we have many members in one body and all the members do not have the same function, so we who are many, are one body in Christ, and individually members one of another. And since we have gifts that differ according to the grace given to us, let each exercise them accordingly: (Rom. 12:4-6A)

\#   \#   \#   \#

Maurice (Maury) A. Johnson

———ANGELS?

We were mired, right to the hubs! We had left the blacktop to drive to Glass Buttes in central Oregon to look for obsidian. Our two-wheel drive van had broken through the crust and underneath was near liquid mud. For some five hours, I had jacked up the car, chained up and stuffed the scant brush and few rocks we could find under the wheels. All to no avail. As darkness approached, we trudged to the highway, uttering not a few prayers.

For about an hour, drivers of passing cars and trucks would take one look at our muddy, disreputable appearance and immediately speed up. Finally, two young men in a four-wheel drive jeep that was as dirty as Happy-Toes and me stopped. These happy young men towed our van out of the mire. After we gave them our heart-felt thanks, we offered to pay them for their trouble.

"Oh no," they said, "We're Christians."

Angels? They were to us.

#   #   #   #

————GOOD SCENTS

We had just deplaned at the Honolulu airport when Happy-Toes exclaimed, "Oh, what wonderful perfume!"

The scent was from the abundance of flowers on the island. Surely, Oahu must be one of God's favorite gardens. Even at Waikiki the smell of the blooms seemed to overpower the diesel exhaust fumes from the buses.

I had been to the Islands several times before when I was in the Naval Air Reserve. Part of our training syllabus required long over-water flights. I had, however, forgotten how great the Sandwich Islands smelled.

As I am writing this, Happy-Toes is baking Christmas cookies and the beautiful scents of cardamon and anise fill the air. I love to soak up those lovely odors.

Thank you Lord for the sense of smell and I look forward to the lovely aromas of Heaven.

For we are a fragrance of Christ to God among those who are being saved and among those who are perishing; (2 Cot. 2:15)

\#   \#   \#   \#

Maurice (Maury) A. Johnson

——GRUMPY OLD MAN

I am not exactly a ray of sunshine when I awake each morning. After two mugs of coffee, I still fumble, stumble and mumble for an hour or so. I am definitely not a morning person.

Some years ago while I was still in the workaday world, I would stumble down our driveway to catch my ride to work. A foster child who the neighbors cared for would be catching a school bus at the same time. Her cheery "Good Morning" and bright smile would generally wake me up.

If you are one who wakes up bright-eyed and bushy-tailed in the morning and you run across a grumpy old man like me, give him a smile and a good morning. Maybe he'll degrump.

> *"Though I say, 'I will forget my complaint, I will leave off my sad countenance and be cheerful. (Job 9:27)*

#   #   #   #

———DECISIONS

"Don't make me decide dad, you tell me what to do," our 12-year-old daughter sobbed.

Judy had a problem. Her confirmation class met on Saturday morning and her junior high Home Ec teacher was taking a group of girls to shop in a nearby city at the same time.

In line with our belief that we should bring up a child in the way he/she should go (Prov.22:6), we had just let the apron-string get longer. I don't remember what the decision was but it was a tough one! What ever it was, Happy-Toes and I stood by it.

We all have decisions to make often; good or bad, spirit or flesh. Paul talks about it in Galatians.

But I say, walk by the Spirit, and you will not carry out the desire of the flesh. For the flesh sets its desire against the Spirit, and the Spirit against the flesh; for they are in opposition to one another, so that you may not do the things that you please. Gal. 5:16, 17

\#   \#   \#   \#

────PEACEMAKERS

President Clinton sent 20,000 of our troops into Bosnia as peacekeepers. That's what I call inflation. You see, 21 of us were supposed to do that in 1945, but let me explain.

It was more than 50 years ago. We had won the war in Europe and our squadron was tabbed for occupation duty so we had to wait for replacements before we could go home. After a flurry of flying ground troops from Italy to Casablanca to catch ships bound for home, we young adventurous combat aircrew types were getting restless. Quite a few of us volunteered for duty in the Pacific, but that war was winding down too.

Twenty-one of us were formed into a riot squad to keep the peace in upcoming elections in Italy and Yugoslavia. In Yugoslavia, the British artillery were in place in the Udine, a hill area above Trieste, the capitol city.

Our unit consisted of a Lieutenant and 20 of us Tech and Staff Sergeants. We were all combat aircrew gunners and were chosen for our proficiency with firearms and explosives. I believe a bigger reason was to keep us out of trouble.

Serbia, Bosnia and Croatia were part of Yugoslavia at that time but have since broken away into separate republics. Two figures were vying for power. Tito (Josef Broz) headed up the Guerillas but I can't remember who led the Partisans. Both of these renegade outfits had assisted our airmen who were shot down in the German-occupied country.

Our efforts were expected to ensure free elections in the area. There were 21 of us. I kind of felt like I was one of the troops at Jericho.

> *Blessed are the peacemakers, for they shall be called sons of God.* Matt. 5:9.

#   #   #   #

———BLOOD

There was a time when the sight of blood made me kind of queasy, especially if it was mine. I did lose quite a bit of it in my childhood and youth, but not on purpose. The blood I shed did no one any good, least of all me.

Blood is very important to God. The life of the flesh is in the blood (Lev.17:11). The blood sign preserved Israel's first born in the land of Egypt (Ex.12:1-13). The blood of sacrificed animals became a temporary covering of sin for the Old Testament saints.

The killing of God's Son furnished a permanent blood eraser for our past sins. When we call upon the name of Jesus, God the Father completely scrubs out those sins and promptly forgets them. If God forgets them, shouldn't we?

> *"For I will forgive their iniquity, and their sin I will remember no more. "*Jer.31:34b

# # # #

212

———ON THE INSIDE

It was raining and Happy-Toes and I were to meet a daughter and her two sons at the mall. I was wearing my trenchcoat and a brimmed hat.

As we neared them, I heard young Kyle say, "Here comes grandpa and he's wearing his detective suit." I hope he wasn't comparing me to Lieutenant Columbo.

We tend to judge people by their outward appearance while our Lord looks at the inside, the heart. Anyway, I don't think the disciples were wearing tuxedos when He called them.

> *For this reason I say to you, do not be anxious*
> *for your life, as to what you shall eat, or what*
> *You shall drink; nor for your body, as to what*
> *you shall put on. Is not life more than food,*
> *and the body than clothing? (Matt. 6:26)*

# # # #

213

———TOYS

We've all seen the bumper sticker that says, "The one that dies with the most toys, wins." I saw a variation of that the other day that said, "The one that dies with the most toys—still dies." Toys like boats, airplanes, etc are neat things, but—. The but is this. We spend more time working on those things than having fun with them. My neighbors with RVs sure do. The trouble with many possessions is that they possess you.

I've got to go now. I have to wash my boat.

And all those who had believed were together, and had all things in common; and they began selling their property and possessions, and were sharing them with all, as anyone might have need. (Acts 2:44, 45)

#   #   #   #

———CHANGE

Have you ever worshiped in a congregation where some people just turned you off? Maybe their attitudes or mannerisms bugged you? Boy, I sure have! Counting the congregation my parents were members of when I was a child, I've been a member of five of them. Over the years, as we have moved we have joined nearby Christian congregations.   Each time, there time there have been people there that I would rather not know too well—until now.

Do you suppose the Lord has changed me?

> *For the Holy Spirit, God's gift, does not want*
> *you to be afraid of people, but to be wise and*
> *strong, and to love them and enjoy being with*
> *them. (2 Tim. 1:7 LB)*

#   #   #   #

Maurice (Maury) A. Johnson

———EARLY TRAINING

Train up a child in the way he should go, even when he Is old he will not depart from it —
Prov. 22:6

Pastor Dave got a call late one night from a dying 84 year old man. He asked if the pastor would come and see him. Dave dressed immediately, grabbed his bible and communion kit and rushed to the bedside.

The man had completed his confirmation class 70 years before. He had gotten mad at the pastor and left, never to darken a church door again.

As Dave read to him from the Bible and talked to him, he was astounded that the man remembered the Lord's prayer and much of the Apostle's Creed. As pastor recounted our Savior's great love for us, the man accepted His salvation. After Holy Communion, Dave told him to put his hand in the hand of Jesus and he did.

P.S. The man's wife, who had never been in a church accepted the Lord that night.

#   #   #   #

——————SPIRITUAL FOOD

I'm big on the four basic food groups; Hershey, Dairy Queen, Burger King and KFC. Happy-Toes feels differently. She believes that veggies belong in there somewhere, so much so, that I often fear for vegetable poisoning after some of our meals.

I do steer away from spiritual junk food, however. There is a lot of that surrounding us. Take most books, movies and television programs, for instance. Most of them are nothing more than artery-cloggers for the spirit.

I enjoy good music, mostly Christian books and a very rare movie. I choose my "food" very carefully. After all, my spirit is going to be around forever and I want it to be healthy.

> *And now, brothers, as I close this letter let me say this one more thing: Fix your thoughts on what is true and good and right. Think about things that are pure and lovely, and dwell on the fine, good things in others. Think about all you can praise God for and be glad about. (Phil 4:8)*

#   #   #   #

217

————PLAIN FOOD

Happy-Toes asked what ai would like for dinner on our fiftieth anniversary. I told her that I would love a plate of boiled navy beans with lots of catsup. She didn't think that was gourmet food so we compromised and ate out. On my birthdays, I order macaroni and cheese. On HTs, we eat out. Another of my treats is white rice with raisins, cinnamon, milk and sugar on it. By now, you know that I like plain food.

When it comes to Bible study, I like plain food, too! Those lofty debates are a real pain. God's word is not to be twisted. The people of the "Jesus Seminar," as well as some theologians in high places in denominations, and their lies will be damned by God if we don't.

Jesus didn't think too highly of the theologians of His day either.

> *"But woe to you, scribes and Pharisees, hypocrites, because you shut off the Kingdom of Heaven from men; for you do not enter in yourselves, nor do you allow those who are entering to go in." Matt; 23:13*

#   #   #   #

Special to the Grapevine

MAURY'S MUSING—HEAVENLY UNION

"Fifty-five years, are you sure, asked Happy-Toes?"

"Yep, it will be in September," I replied.

"I've kinda gotten used to you by now," said she, "I'd like to keep you forever now that I've got you broken in."

"Let's see what Jesus has to say about that," I replied.

At first, two statements by our Lord seem to contradict each other. As we look more closely, we see that they are compatible. In Matthew 22:30, our Lord tells us, "For in the resurrection they neither marry, nor are given in marriage, but are like angels in heaven." In Matthew 16:19 and again in Matthew 18:18, He tells us that whatever we bind on earth will be bound in Heaven. Happy-Toes and I bound each other our troth many years ago.

Besides being man and wife here on earth, we are brother and sister in the kingdom of God. We are also members of The Church and are therefore collectively the bride of Christ. There is no need to populate Heaven so there is no procreation there. We will be neuters. The sexual process which has caused so much sin on earth will no longer exist. Don't worry, God has prepared heavenly delights that far surpass those on earth!

"Yes, as brother and sister, we can live together and you can still tell me when I need a haircut."

*   *   *   *   *

Maurice (Maury) A. Johnson

Special to the Grapevine.

MAURY'S MUSING—ON FOOD.

"This article in the Sunday paper says that potatoes are not good for you", said Happy-Toes.

"The writer must be the same character that keeps saying that coffee and chocolate are bummers, too", said I. "You sure can tell the author isn't a Norwegian, Irishman or German!"

I think perhaps that people who don't like a particular food tend to think that it isn't good for anyone. There are whole denominations based on what foods are forbidden to eat. I thought it best to appeal to a higher authority. In Paul's letter to Timothy, he says:

"For everything created by God is good, and nothing is to be rejected, if it is to be received with gratitude; for it is sanctified by means of the word of God and prayer."
—1 Timothy 4:4,5.

"Aw, c'mon Happy-Toes, not broccoli tonight, you know it's not good for me."

*   *   *   *   *

MAURY'S MUSING—ON THE MIND.

Happy-Toes placed the phone on the hook and looked at me. "I forgot that we had an appointment to have our pictures taken for the church directory. Am I getting Alzheimers?"

"Definitely not," I replied, "but at 74, you may have old-timers!"

Our brain is like our computers in that we can never completely get rid of information this side of Heaven. The data are all hidden there somewhere taking up space. We just have an awful lot of garbage stored in our craniums. We have junk that comes from TV, books, movies, radio and magazines that is absolutely useless.

Science tells us that even a great mind like Albert Einstein only operated at about 10 percent capacity. Evidently, his head was cluttered, too. I figure that television producers must operate on a below-zero scale.

When we get to Heaven, either via the death of our bodies or at the rapture, all that garbage we've collected will be left behind. The Sanctification* that began when we accepted the Lord's gift will be complete.

During the Millenium, when we have 100 % of our God-given brains in use, think of what we will be able to accomplish! Sorry folks, you will definitely not lay around on clouds playing the harp all day. The best part is that we will be able to worship God with a full mind as well as a clean heart.

Maurice (Maury) A. Johnson

> *"For behold, I create new heavens and a new earth; and the former things shall not be remembered or come to mind." (Isa. 65:17)*

*   *   *   *   *

* Sanctify means to make holy or to free from sin.

———TIME

Before the mountains were brought forth,
or ever Thou hadst formed
Earth and the world even from everlastin
to everlasting,
Thou art God. (Psa. 90:2)

It sure is hard to think of anything being everlasting! Especially when that toaster quits after a year or we realize that our automobile will never see 20 years.

We are creatures that live by the clock. The alarm clock tells us when to rise. There's a time to eat, a time to go to school or work and even a time to die. (Eccles. 3:2)

Perhaps, it's easier to think of eternity as the absence of time. Time is a creation of God and did not exist until He set the planets in motion! Our Creator tells us that Him a day or a thousand years are the same. (Psa. 90:4) (2 Peter 3:8)

No, there won't be a Timex in all of Heaven. Oh, and one other thing, in Heaven, I can't be late to anything.

#   #   #   #

Maurice (Maury) A. Johnson

————NAMES

As I looked at the surnames on the back of the jerseys, I wondered how these names began or how they evolved. Take Favre for instance, the MVP quarterback of the Packers. It sounds French but I am limited in that language as I haven't spoken it in 57 years. My name is easy. Johnson means son of John. Nearly every Swede that came to this country became a Johnson. My friend Reuben Ben Yonatan is easy, too. In English, he is Reuben, son of Jonathon.

One of the reasons that many people shy away from the study of last days prophesy is the strange names. Names like Gomer, Magog, Put and Lud don't mean much to most people. Many of these names were the grandsons of Noah. By finding out where they settled after the flood we can solve some mysteries.

Persia is easy to find. It includes Iran, Iraq and part of Mesopotamia. Babylon is in Iraq and Put is Libya. Lud became Ethiopia and Gomer is Germany. The old USSR and Turkey are represented by Magog, Meshech and Tubal.

Keep these areas in mind as you read your news magazines. Often you can read Bibical prophesy coming to life.

Another reason for right living is this: you know how late it is; time is running out. Wake up, for the coming of the Lord is nearer now than when we first believed (Romans 13:11)

\#   \#   \#   \#

224

———BODY OF CHRIST

There is nothing worse than a toothache, well, maybe an earache. I've had some dandy toothaches in my day, hurts that had me banging my head against a wall. However, I haven't had one cavity since I started using Dentu-creme.

We, who are Christians, are all members of the body of Christ. I figure I'm a tooth, ear or a toenail because I've given the Lord so much trouble in my lifetime. We are not all mouths (preachers) nor are we all feet (missionaries) but we all have a part in God's plan. Perhaps we are helping hands to give aid to a stranger or neighbor. I guess if we don't do our job, it just won't get done.

> *Now here is what I am trying to say: All of you together are the one body of Christ and each one of you is a separate and necessary part of it. (1 Cor. 12:27 LB)*

#   #   #   #

———EYES

"She's at it again, son," my dad said.

Mom had been acting strangely. She had insisted that Dad paint the interior of their home, again, complaining that it looked dingy. She had sent her clothes to the cleaners for the second time in a month and had rewashed all Dad's work clothes before he had a chance to wear them.

Luckily, she was soon due for her annual eye exam. The doctor found that Mom had cataracts. When they were removed, the whole world brightened up. Just in time, too. Another six months and Mom would have shot their budget for a long time on cleaning bills and paint.

We seem to have spiritual cataracts until we accept God's grace. Then, it's like scales are removed from our eyes and our whole world brightens up.

> *I pray that your hearts will be flooded with light so that you can see something of the future He has called you to share. I want you to realize that God has been made rich because we who are Christ's have been given to Him! (Eph. 1:18)*

#   #   #   #

———NEIGHBORS

As I write this, our weather people have issued a warning for gale force winds. No, these winds are not coming from Washington D. C. this time. The storm is supposed to hit the west coast of the U.S. later today.

We have residents as old as 95 in our senior mobile home court. As we are in an all-electric area, we lose heating and cooking facilities when our power fails. Several of us youngsters (75-year-olds) have prepared for such an emergency and we have agreed to check on our neighbors. We have wood or propane stoves, kerosene lamps and camp stoves so no one should be cold or hungry.

This is a grand way to get to know your neighbors. If adversity comes your way, throw a party! Pass the canned beans, please.

We remember the second of our new commandments.

"You shall love your neighbor as yourself."
Matt. 22:39.

#   #   #   #

Maurice (Maury) A. Johnson

———SICK

Oh mercy I was sick! First, I was afraid I'd die, and then I was afraid I wouldn't. I had been very ill before. I'd had malaria, near burst appendix and various other problems, but nothing like this! It never should have happened to me, a guy that back-seated dive bombers, flew through huge flak parties and spent 22 years flying in rain squalls looking for submarines.

It all started with a notice on our workplace bulletin board. I signed up, paid my fee and found myself on a bus at 4:30 a.m. heading for a local deep-sea port for our salmon fishing charter.

My breakfast at the greasy-spoon restaurant consisted of oatmeal and toast as I wanted a gentle stomach. I hadn't drunk any of the beer on the bus that so many had. In short, I had taken every precaution except Dramamine.

The Coast Guard hadn't allowed the charter boats out of the harbor the previous three days because of rough seas and we awaited their decision this day. It was "go" with a possible recall.

The 75-foot boat tossed in the trough and was precisely positioned to trap the diesel exhaust from the two Caterpillar engines in the half-cabin. I had company as I hung over the side yelling for ROARKE and chumming for fish. I couldn't enjoy the beauty of the salmon I caught.

A lot of people are going to be sicker than I was when they realize that the Lord has called the Christians out of this world and they failed to take advantage of the opportunity to go with them.

#   #   #   #

228

————CHARGING MY BATTERY

For many years it was my dream to have a car that had a good battery. I think I spent half my life with a dead battery, both me and my auto. In those days, we didn't have automatic transmissions and I was always looking for a hill to park on. By rolling a bit and popping the clutch in second gear, the car would generally start.

Now that I can afford a good battery for the car, the only one I have to worry about is mine. Although I try to keep plugged in to God's energy system all the time, my engine runs a lot better if I get my battery charged each week at Sunday services. I get that extra energy for my system when I worship the Lord with other believers.

#   #   #   #

Maurice (Maury) A. Johnson

———BAND-AIDS

Happy-Toes is a quilter. She caught the quilting bug some 25 years ago and has warmed family and friends with more than a hundred of her covers. She is finishing a flower garden now. It looks like a thousand little hexagons, hand sewn together and hand quilted.

As a result of all this sewing, she sometimes wears band-aids on her fingers. One day after preparing meat loaves for us and for her mother, she noticed that a band-aid was missing from her thumb. It was nowhere to be found. She called Gram.

"Mom, look for a surprise in your meatloaf," she said, telling her the story.

Gram called later. "It didn't affect the taste one bit."

Into each life some band-aid must fall. Did you know that there is a verse for quilters in the Bible?

> *A time to tear apart, and a time to sew together. Eccles. 3:7*

#   #   #   #

———KINFOLK

"How about going to the Golden Mum for a Chinese dinner tonight," said Happy-Toes? We have a great variety of ethnic restaurants in our area and we enjoy most of them. Oh, I wouldn't choose the spicy Thai food for everyday eating. Although I like all the ingredients in Mexican chow, I always get the feeling that there are people in the back room that prechew the food for me. I love the great southern barbeque ribs and Italian spaghetti. Chinese-American food is always a treat. For everyday eating though, I'll take Irish grub. The corned beef and cabbage, Irish stew and shepherd's pie suit me just fine.

As the old poor-man's philosopher thought about this, I realized that I am related to each of these ethnic groups. No wonder I enjoy the vittles of all these peoples, for we are kinfolks. We share great, great (many times) grandparents. You see, we are all related to Adam and Noah and therefore each other.

Today is Martin Luther King, Jr. Day and I mused. How can anyone show dislike for their brothers and sisters?

#   #   #   #

Maurice (Maury) A. Johnson

———REUNION

Happy-Toes and I are not big on television. We watch mainly news, music specials and sporting events. HT likes one game show and we watch science news. We heard about an afternoon program on which four brothers who had been adopted out to different families as babies would be reunited. We watched this very emotional experience. When we learned that through that program, the birth mother had been located and would be reunited with them at a later episode, we had to watch.

The mother told of extreme hardship and that she had longed for those kids every day for the 37 years that they had been gone. The reunion was glorious!

I separated myself from my Father God when I was a teenager. It was much later when this prodigal returned to Him. You know, He longed for me while I was gone. We too, had a glorious reunion!

#   #   #   #

———REVIVAL, APOSTASY

Each Spring we practice the ancient ritual of (ugh) housecleaning. It is a time when we get rid of dust, dirt and a whole bunch of stuff we've collected but don't need. Then we spruce up our yards and houses with plantings and paint for the coming summer.

God is doing much the same thing with His church for His coming thousand year summer here on earth. Apostate or false teachers are dusting away from the faith of many who are borderline believers.

> Matt. 24:24 *For false Christs and false prophets will arise And will show great signs and wonders, so as to mislead, if possible, even the elect.*

At the same time, our Lord is painting true believers with the Holy Spirit much as in the time of Acts! We are seeing great revivals in Africa, South America and the former USSR. The Spirit of God is starting to show in the Orient. As yet, the West seems relatively untouched.

> Acts 2:17,18 *"And it shall be in the last days," God says," that I will pour forth of My Spirit upon all mankind; and your sons and your daughters shall prophesy and your young men shall see visions, and your old men shall dream dreams; Even upon my bondslaves, both men and women, I will pour Forth of my spirit and they shall prophesy.*

Maurice (Maury) A. Johnson

Apostasy and revival. Just two of the many signs of the last days.

\#   \#   \#   \#.

——————JUDGEMENT DAY

The church I attended as a young boy was big on judgement day. I got the feeling that nobody, but nobody, could live up to God's standards. I could see myself standing before the judgement seat. The Lord would point at me and would say, "Little Maury, you've played baseball on Sunday, you've lied to your parents and you smoked Bull Durham behind the barn! Be consigned to the deepest part of The Lake of Fire!

I figured I'd have plenty of company there because I had friends that had tasted beer, gone to movies, dances and even played cards. There were a great many man-made laws of Christianity, then.

It was years later before I realized how wonderful God is. He loves me so much that He let His own Son die for my sins so that I don't have to. Think of it, we have a God who gives us laws for successful living, then pays our fine when we can't keep them!

There is a judgement day for the unbeliever. (2 Peter 3:7) The judgement day for the believer is more of an awards ceremony where we will receive crowns. A martyr's crown (Rev. 2:10), one for faithful ministers (1 Peter 5:4), and one for soul winners (Phil. 4:1) (1 Thess. 2:19).

The one I'll get for sure is the one given to those who are looking forward to Christ's return.

> 2 Tim. 4:8: *In the future there is laid up for me the crown of Righteousness, which the Lord, the righteous judge, will award To me on that*

Maurice (Maury) A. Johnson

day; and not only to me, but also to all who have Loved His appearing.

# # # #

———JAILBIRD

Perhaps I should call this bit, "Memoirs of a Jailbird." I did time in the maximum security guardhouse at Biggs Field, El Paso, Texas. Let me tell you about the hard-time I did.

It was 1944. I had finished aerial gunnery school and I was awaiting an assignment to an aircrew and overseas deployment. Happy-Toes and I, recently married, lived off base. I would check daily at the field for my orders. Our barracks was one of a jillion cookie-cutter two story buildings that were thrown up during WW2 to house we citizen soldiers. I tossed my hat on my bunk and went to the next barracks, hatless, 75 feet away to check my mail.

As I sauntered to the Post Office, I was seen by the Provost Marshall who was passing by in a jeep. My crime was not being covered when outdoors.

The iron-bar door clanked shut behind me and I surveyed the situation. The large second floor was one room. It housed 80-90 men, mostly hard cases. There were lawbreakers of every stripe, murderers and rapists. Kangaroo courts were common. Great fights took place and home-made knives flashed in the blood splattered restroom as many toughs vied to be boss.

I knew that I couldn't be held more than 24 hours unless charges were filed. Promptly at that time, I rattled that barred door and called for the Corporal of the Guard.

When I left the front door of the guardhouse into the fresh air and sunshine, I heaved a sigh of relief. I had just had a small taste of hell. I imagine the world will be left like that when we Christians are taken to Heaven via the Rapture.

#   #   #   #

———HOUSE OF BREAD

The little town's name meant House of Bread. It was a fitting name for a sleepy town nestled in the rolling hills of farm country. Once, it had been the hometown of Ruth and Boaz. One boy, who was raised here, became a highly regarded king of the country. His name was David.

Each year, a great number of tourists, passing through, swarmed into the village. The surrounding area was sheep country and people would buy the lambs they would sacrifice at Passover in Jerusalem, just six miles north. More than 100,000 lambs would be purchased for sacrifices each year.

We know it's name as Bethlehem, where the ultimate Passover Lamb was born.

For there is born to you this day in the city of David a Savior, who is Christ the Lord.
(Luke 2:11)

#   #   #   #

———LONGEVITY

My folks wouldn't have been caught dead in a senior center. "Too many old folks there," they said.

Maybe they had something. Mom passed away at 89 and Dad at 92 when illness overtook them. Happy-Toes and I both come from long-lived families. Her mother lived to be 96 and I had a grandad that would have made 97 if he had lived 20 more days. Why do our families live so long? I know many people who retired at 65, plunked themselves down in front of the TV and died soon. Maybe we can find a common thread in the lives of those who lived so long.

Most of my examples loved the Lord. All of them loved their families and their neighbors. All of them would lend a hand to anyone who needed one. My mother-in-law was famous for her calls and cards to the bereaved and sick. Each of them had many interests. They were all young at heart! Oh yes, they all heeded Ex. 20:12:

> *Honor your father and your mother, that your days may be Long on the land which the Lord your God is giving you.*

# # # #

──────WISDOM

Wisdom is a commodity reserved for the elderly. It is Earned by a good life well lived.
John Carlson.

It's hard to believe that quote came from a 31 year old radio talk show host. He should be very wise indeed when he gets old.

I've admired the wisdom of the elderly ever since I grew out of my teenage smartdom. I prayed for wisdom and with it understanding. I'm only 76, but when I get old I expect to get my wish. Yes, the sage pearls of the older folks are to be treasured.

*How much better to get wisdom than gold! And to get understanding is to be chosen rather then silver. (*Prov.16:16)

And we know where wisdom begins.

*The fear of the Lord is the beginning of wisdom; a good Understanding have all those who do His commandments. His praise endures forever. (*Psa.111:10)

#   #   #   #

———POWERED FLIGHT

It is the year 2003 and we are celebrating 100 years of powered flight. I think back some 60 years to my first experience in the air. The beginning was a flight in a J 3 Piper Cub. A little more than a year later, I with six other 19-21 year-olds climbed into a Flying Fortress and flew to Europe to take part in an air war. It was quite an adventure for a farm boy.

Prophets of old had seen these marvelous flying machines. About 2600 years ago, the prophet Isaiah, telling about the end days and the return of the Jews from the diaspora (scattering) saw aircraft.

> *And what do I see flying like clouds to Israel, like doves to their nests? They are the ships of Tarshish, reserved to bring the people of Israel home. (Isaiah 60:8)*

#   #   #   #

242

————A PSALM OF PRAISE

At our Bible study, we are reading through the Bible. As we near the center chapter, (it's Psa. 117), Pastor Jeff challenged us to write a Psalm. This is my Psalm of praise.

We offer our praise and all of creation
Joins in with blossom and bloom,
And feather and song,
With light and with color,
With sight and with scent,
And gentle rain and warming sun.
Our worship competes with
The glory of nature and it seems that
Words fall short when tested this way.
But, praise with love and service with heart will
Always be precious to God!
He reminds us we are royal priests
And our worship is like lustrous pearls to Him.

Maury.

Maurice (Maury) A. Johnson

————PSALM OF AFFLICTION

I enjoyed writing a praise psalm and wrote another, about pain. If you'd like to try writing one, just be honest about your feelings and use your own words.

Pain is a presence that strikes as it will,
And seeks to destroy parasitic the soul.
Like an arrow so sharp, it sticks in the flesh
And mirrors itself to double and more.
Like sword and like club it leaves it's effects
And shadows.
But pain meets it's match by peace in the soul
And, that peace is a gift from the Savior.
It flows and it floods over the heart and
Calms the spirit.
It reminds me that
Pain will be no more when I cross that
Valley and am escorted to the Tree of Life
Whose leaves are for healing.

                              Maury

————WHAT'S IN A NAME?

I just had my hair shampooed with Exotic Orchid petals, or so it said on the bottle. When we had our house painted last, it was with Jonquil Sunrise.

The Madison Avenue types seem to think we are more apt to buy a product if it has an appealing name. To me, it doesn't make any difference if that paint name is Jonquil Sunrise or light yellow. I don't suppose I'd like Baby Diaper Yellow, though. As for shampoo, we buy the one that is on sale and we don't buy it for the name.

I wonder how Madison Avenue would dress up salvation. What kind of terms would they use? They don't have to gussie it up for me. I'll take it in the words of John 1:11-12:

> *He came to His own, and His own did not receive Him. But as many as received Him, He gave the right to become Children of God, to those who believe in His name.*

#   #   #   #

Maurice (Maury) A. Johnson

————MERCIES.

I had retired for the second time. As I went on my walk to the Post Office several blocks away, I passed a church that volunteers were painting. I went home, put on some old clothes, grabbed some paint tools and joined them.

As I was painting, the maintenance director of the local school district offered me a job. Thinking about the "food baby" I had grown while jockeying a desk for some years, I accepted. Thus began another career, painting.

It was summer vacation time for the kids and I was painting in a big, old high school. I'd set up my paint shop in the dirt floor portion of the school's basement. I was a little behind in my self-imposed schedule because we had taken a day off the previous week to update our first aid training.

Should I or shouldn't I? Should I spend part of my 20 minute lunch break climbing the two flights of stairs and taking the long walk to eat with my friend in the janitor's room? I could just plunk my hind end down on my make-shift work bench and eat there. For some reason, I chose the former.

As I entered the janitor's office, he was liver colored, slumped in a chair and nearly out of it. I pointed at my throat. His nearly imperceptible nod told me all I needed to know. Grabbing him from his chair, I administered the newly learned Heimlich maneuver.

The rolled up piece of sandwich meat fell to the floor and my friend gasped for air to fill his lungs. I wondered. Why was I there against all odds with a newly discovered, first aid method?

246

The Lord is good to all, and His mercies are over All His works. Psa. 145:9

#   #   #   #

Maurice (Maury) A. Johnson

————ALL IN THE FAMILY

Happy-Toes and I have four children. Those four have nine and two of them have our four great-grandchildren. A son-in-law has four kids by a previous marriage as well as two grandkids. When we add in my wife's two sisters and five nieces and nephews, their 15 children and a bunch of spouses, we can throw a dandy family picnic! My late brother had five kids and they are all prolific. I'll not count a great many cousins, some of which I have outlived.

Our extended family is long on love and are about 96% Christian. Our church congregations vary and include several denominations. On special occasions we worship with each other. As the oldest geezer of this tribe, I've had to assume the role of patriarch, a job similar to shepherd.

God has families, too. Many centuries ago, Jehovah chose Israel to be His wife. She was picked to keep God's word true and to furnish the mother of His Son. She has been unfaithful and God has punished her many times. The seven-year tribulation period punishment will bring her back to God for good.

Many people mix the two families of God, mentally. There is a great difference. The church is the bride of Christ. He purchased us with His blood. As His bride, we will be raptured before the tribulation, leaving God to deal with the Jews, during that seven years.

For Christ has accomplished the whole purpose of the law. All who believe in Him are made right with God. (Rom. 10:4)

And so all Israel will be saved. Do you remember what the prophets said about this? A deliverer will come from Jerusalem, and He will turn Israel from all ungodliness, and then I will keep my covenant with them and take away their sins. (Rom. 12:26,27)

#   #   #   #

Maurice (Maury) A. Johnson

———LOST SOULS

If you are as old as I am, you may remember an old radio program entitled, "Mr. Keene Tracer of Lost Persons." Our hero would find lost loves, relatives and old friends. My personal computer (PC) is a keen tracer of lost persons too. Through it I have access to telephone directories and many other sources of information.

I have had a good deal of enjoyment finding lost relatives, old Army buddies, and missing friends for my neighbors. It's heart-warming to be told of reunions that take place because of my searches.

A couple of years ago, I was approached by a friend and asked to find her "lost" son. Let's call my friend Lucy. While a young girl, she had given birth to an illegitimate son and had given him up for adoption.

"Is he alive, is he well, can you find him," she asked? I collected all the clues she could give me and I headed for the World-Wide Web.

When I handed Lucy a sheet of paper with her son's name, address and phone number on it, she trembled. The weeks and months went by but Lucy didn't write or call the man. She was afraid of being rejected.

A few months went by and Lucy unexpectedly died of a heart attack. She never got to know her son.

I expect a lot of people are like Lucy when it comes to their salvation. They just put off coming to the Lord and claiming the freebee that He paid for at the cross. It's sad to think that some will know about the Son, but never knowing Him personally.

# # # #

———GRAY HAIR.

When we were in Scandinavia, we were amazed to see that apparently no one there has gray hair. It appears that when people get older over there, their hair turns red instead of gray! It turns kind of a henna color. It must be their water.

We live near a high school and many boys and girls have weird colored mops, greens, purples, etc. Last night on TV I saw a lady who had managed to dye her hair roots black without staining her lovely blond hair.

In a TV commercial, a man transforms his crown from gray to a youthful brown with a product called Grecian Formula. If I went after that with my memory, I would probably bring home Roman Formula by mistake and turn my hair weird like those high school kids.

Our Lord associates gray hair with wisdom and righteousness so I'll leave mine as it is.

The silver-haired head is a crown of glory, If it is found in the way of righteousness.
Prov. 16:31

\#　\#　\#　\#

Maurice (Maury) A. Johnson

MAURY'S MUSING—THE WORST DAY

"We are in not too bad shape for the shape we're in," said Happy-Toes.

We were taking inventory of our aches and pains. I had been to a chiropractor who'd gotten rid of some of my back and leg pains. The last few years had not been kind to Happy-Toes and me in the pain department but our sufferings are minor when we think of our Lord's travail. Death by crucifixion is terrible even without piling the sins of Hitler, Stalin, Idi Amin and me on our Lord. Could anything be worse?

Yes, the Lord's worst day is yet to come! It is a time at the end of the Millennium when all the unsaved must pass before Jesus as judge and receive the verdict, "Guilty." It is doubly painful when we realize that He forgave them all, they just didn't pick up their pardon.

> *"For as the Father has life in Himself, so He*
> *has granted the Son to have life in Himself and*
> *has given Him authority to Execute judgement*
> *also because He is the Son of Man.*
> John 5:26, 27.

Dear Jesus, I ask you to forgive my sins. Thank you. Amen.

252

MAURY'S MUSING—ON THE HEART

Everything was fuzzy. Objects on the ceiling and upper wall were not a bit distinct. During the moments when I was semi-awake, I tried to figure out where I was.

"The doctor said the operation went fine," said Happy-Toes as she held a cold compress to my forehead.

In a couple of hours the eminent surgeon came in and sat down. "Your main aortic valve is now a bovine valve as the pig valves were not big enough. You also have three bypasses."

That's great, I thought, the bovine valve is more apt to be kosher than the pig part.

Later, I allowed as how that valve must have come out of a raging, dust-pawing rodeo bull like one of our sons-in-law rode. Happy-Toes didn't think so. She thought it probably came out of Ferdinand, the bull of song who liked to smell the posies. Maybe she's right.

My heart is working although it does have kind of a weird rhumba beat. Our Lord isn't interested in odd rhythms but he does judge us by our heart. (1 Sam. 16:7) Is it loving and generous? Let us say with David:

> *"Create in me a clean heart, Oh God, and renew a steadfast spirit within me."*
> Psalm 51:10

*   *   *   *   *

Maurice (Maury) A. Johnson

MAURY'S MUSING—THE LONELIEST CHRISTMAS

Have you ever been lonely in a crowd? I sure have. The year was 1946 and the day was Christmas.

World War 2 had been over for a few months and although I had ample "points" to come home, the 96th Bomb Squadron had been tapped for occupation duty. I had to wait until a new Flight Engineer/Gunner was sent to Italy to replace me.

Finally my replacement came and I boarded the USS Monterey in Naples harbor, headed for home. The aircraft carrier had been modified for use as a troopship. I seem to remember that 4500 of us were accommodated in compartments and the six-tiers of bunks on the hangar deck.

After losing so many comrades in the long war, we were reluctant to make more short-term friendships. Our thoughts turned inward as our visions were of home and hearth. Here we were in the midst of 4,499 others, spending the loneliest day of our lives.

I believe there were Christmas services on the ship but I didn't know about them. My Christmas dinner was interrupted as the ship lurched and the legs of the mess table where I was seated collapsed. My dinner and a pitcher of coffee soaked into my last clean uniform.

I made my way to the ship's fan-tail so I could breath air that was clear of the odor of sea-sickness that filled my assigned compartment. We were in the mid-Atlantic in the middle of winter.

Do you know of someone who might be lonely this Christmas? There is probably someone on a nearby military base or a neighbor who would enjoy God's love you could pass on. How about taking somebody to church with you and sharing Christmas dinner.

And do not neglect doing good and sharing;
for with such sacrifices God is pleased.
(Heb. 13:16)

#   #   #   #

Special to the Grapevine.

MAURY'S MUSING—GENERATIONS

I turned off of the main road, pulled into the parking lot of the Grange Hall, which had once been a church and stopped the car. At the request of a relative from California, four of us were here to recall experiences for an video tape about my grandparents, Albert and Christina, and their homestead.

I started the car and followed the driveway into a valley of memories. I pulled up as a 94-year-old uncle, his slightly younger brother and a cousin of mine got out of a car near the house.

In the 1890s, the newlywed Johnsons came from Sweden to the local area to take up a homestead. Following grandpa's priorities, the first order of business was to mark off an acre for a church and another for a school. Then began the back-breaking land clearing and the building of a fine farm.

That tape is played often on our local access channel. Each time I see it, I am reminded of our generations. My wonderful grandparents prayed for us even as Happy-Toes and I pray for our family even for our great-grandchildren. Three or four generations can be cursed (Exodus 20:5), or blessed.

> Isaiah 59:21. *"And as for me, this is my covenant with them," says the Lord: "My Spirit which is upon you, and My words which I have put in your mouth, shall not depart from*

your mouth, nor from the mouth of your offspring, nor from the mouth of your offspring's offspring," says the Lord, "from now and forever."

#   #   #   #

MAURY'S MUSING—CHANGE HISTORY?

"Let's go rescue a damsel in distress, I told my partner as we headed for the patrol car. Several of us senior citizens are police volunteers here in Poulsbo. We issue $250 tickets to people wrongfully parked in handicap parking places and open car doors for folks who have locked in their keys. We check homes for families who are away and patrol schools, residential areas and banks. We come from many backgrounds and have reputations of being able to do most everything from manning the police boat to unsnarling traffic.

We Christians are able to do most everything, too, through prayer, that is! We can rearrange geographical features (Matt. 6:10) and change history (with one caveat).

Seven centuries before our Lord Jesus came to earth, Hezekiah, the King of Judah, was on his deathbed. He was one of the three best Bibical kings and he pleaded with God for more time. God granted him 15 more years. During that time, he sired the most evil king the Israelites ever had and who reigned for 55 years.

That caveat? From the Hezekiah story and from the Lord's prayer, I have learned to add, *"Above all, thy will be done,"* to my prayers. Read more about it in the 14th chapter of Hezekiah and the 20th and 21st chapters of 2 Kings.

#   #   #   #

MAURY'S MUSING—MEMORY?

I suspect that we all have departed friends that we figure we may-or-not-see when we get to Heaven. How can we not have tears (Isa.25:8, Rev.7:17, Rev. 21:4), if we are missing a good buddy or a fine neighbor?

I had two uncles that I dearly loved when I was a boy. They were very good to me. Their wives were lovely Christian ladies, but I don't think either Uncle Claude or Uncle Roy ever darkened a church door. Of course, we all know that attending church does not automatically make a person a Christian. If it did, you'd call me a Toyota when I entered the garage.

Happy-Toes had two aunts she loved and I had a younger brother that I was concerned about. My brother was in elementary school when I went off to war and I saw him very infrequently until his early death.

I hope to see you all in Heaven, but if those dear ones of ours aren't there, we won't have any memory of them.

> Eccles. 9:5,6. *For the living know that They will die; but the dead know nothing, And they have no more reward, for the Memory of them is forgotten. Also their Love, their hatred, and their envy are now Perished; nevermore will they have a share In any thing done under the sun.*
>
> Isa. 26:14 *The dead will not live, the de-Parted spirits will not rise; therefore Thou Hast*

punished and destroyed them, and Thou hast wiped out all remembrance of them.

\#   \#   \#   \#

MAURY'S MUSING—THE BABY!

Things have not been the same at our house since the baby came! Babies have a way of disrupting the most orderly of households and ours is no exception.

Our hearts went out to this little waif and we had to give her a home. Her mother had deserted her when she was only six-weeks old. Now, we have to watch where we walk or sit for baby toys litter the house. However, Happy-Toes did manage to teach the baby to use the sandbox in short order.

Wait a minute—, you didn't think—, nah, we are in our mid seventies. The baby is a kitten, the runt of a litter. Rutabaga Q. Dumpling is the name we gave her. I believe she is second only to God in ruling our household.

I am convinced that God made pets for the express purpose of showing his love to us through these animals. In experiments with pets in nursing homes, their worth has been proved in terms of mental health and happiness.

We have a great many things to thank God for this Thanksgiving. As Happy-Toes and I thank God for each other, our breaths, kin and our church family, we'll also remember to thank Him for God's little fuzzy-faced ambassador.

\#   \#   \#   \#

MAURY'S MUSING—ROSE PETALS

"Grandma Cady was baptized with rose petals, once," said Happy-Toes.

We had been discussing HT's grandma. At the turn of the century, Dolly was the "Belle of the Ball." From ballroom to ballroom, she danced her way to many trophies. In a whirlwind romance, she met and married a dapper star of the Ringling Brothers, Barnum and Bailey Circus that was appearing in Seattle. Oh, the shame of it all! Circus people were not considered to be the most exemplary types.

The union lasted less than a week and Dolly's parents had the marriage annulled. The result of that union was a daughter who was given up for adoption and Dolly resumed her fun times.

Later, Dolly got "religion", rather a series of religions. From one 'storefront church" to another she sought redemption. At each one she was re-saved and re-baptized. At one, she was baptized with rose petals.

Finally, Dolly found the Lord at a revival meeting. She lived her Christianity and spent years feeding "down-and-outers" and passing out Christian literature at night on the streets of Seattle.

In later years, she was widowed and later she became blind. Some one came to her rescue, though. The daughter she had given away some 75 years before took her in and cared for her for many years. That daughter was Happy-Toes' mother.

Matthew 6:12 *"And forgive us our debts, as we also have forgiven our debtors."*

# # # #

262

———UMBRELLA

"It's time to get the patio chairs and umbrella out," said Happy-Toes.

I store those items in the garage during the winter and bring them out when spring is here to stay. The big, blue umbrella that shades our picnic table, shelters us from the hot sun in the afternoon when we visit with friends or eat on the patio. That circle of canvas saves us from a shower sometimes, too.

I know people who believe that the umbrella of church membership is all that's needed to save them, period. Alas, it's not so. Becoming a Christian is a very personal event. It starts with the knowledge that God loves us and that He gave His Son to prove it. We accept that sacrifice and thank Jesus.

Church membership is important for worship and fellowship. It allows us to pool our talents and offerings to share in ministries. It gives us chances to encourage one another. It also carries a promise.

"For where two or three gather together because they are mine, I am there among them." (Matt. 18:20)

\#   \#   \#   \#

263

MAURY'S MUSING—VIVA LA DIFFERENCE

"Our ten grandchildren are all so different." said Happy-Toes. "Each has differing likes and dislikes, occupations and hobbies. And we love them all dearly."

I got to thinking about whole governments and kingdoms that are based on each citizen being practically a clone of the leader. Over the years I've seen many church congregations start that are based on every member thinking and acting alike. Most of them have since fallen by the wayside.

I'd go nuts fast if I had to spend a half-hour with my clone. He'd have a yellow house like ours and drive a red motorcycle and a white Camry. That would be boring! Not only that, he'd be chasing after my wife.

The Christian Church is a group of Saints that are wonderfully diversified. Our Creator made us in all different shapes, sizes and colors. He gave us varying talents while we were yet in the womb and different great gifts when we became His. The genes and DNA marker He gave us were to make sure we didn't bore Him with too much sameness.

Best of all, God loves us with a much greater love than we can muster for our wonderful grandkids.

For I wish that all men were even as I myself. But Each one has his own gift from God, one in this Manner and another in that. (1 Cor. 7:7)

#   #   #   #

———LUGGAGE

"It's not big enough, Dad," said my daughter as she looked at my suitcase.

Our oldest daughter was going to Colorado to visit her son, his wife and a daughter and family for a week of well-deserved vacation. I think she probably needed a bigger bag to hold all the goodies she was taking to her grandkids.

My suitcase will fit in a overhead rack in an airliner. It has wheels and a pull-out handle and it holds enough to last me for 10-12 days, normally. Years ago, I would take a whole bunch of extra stuff in case. However, I learned better before I got stoop-shouldered.

I am looking forward to my next trip. Unlike former trips to Europe, Alaska, etc., this one is out of this world. No, it's not to a man-made space station, and I won't be able to take even my small bag with me because everything I take, has to fit in my heart. I'm glad Doctor Mark said I have a big heart. Well, what he said was that it was enlarged.

The luggage I take will be my nature and character. What will it be? Will I be loving and generous? Maybe I'll be an old grouch. Whatever, we have a few years down here on the earth to develop these things and we'll take them with us to the next higher plane.

There are some things we can send ahead, though!

"Store your treasures in heaven, where they will never become moth-eaten or rusty, and where they will be safe from thieves. Wherever

your treasure is, there your heart and thoughts will also be." (Matt. 6:29,21)

#   #   #   #

————BONE BOX

The first hard evidence of our Savior's existence, other than in our hearts and in Bible accounts, has been found. Oh, early historians, such as Josephus, have told of Jesus, but archeologists are a hard lot to convince of anything. I believe that they are all Thomases at heart.

A bone box, or ossuary, was used to inter (entomb) the bones of one deceased in Jesus' day. At death the body was buried in the ground, normally. The well-to-do had cave tombs that were carved in the limestone but these were the exception. Often the cave had a bench that was hewn from the rock. The corpse was laid on the bench, prepared with spices and left for a year.

After a year, the bones were cleaned and placed in the ossuary. The box was generally carved from limestone and the longest dimension accommodated the leg bones, the body's longest. Sometimes other family members shared the ossuary. Often, geometric designs were carved in the soft stone.

Recently an ossuary was found that has created quite a stir. It was found in a private collection. The inscription reads; *James, son of Joseph, brother of Jesus.*

James was either a half-brother or step-brother of Jesus. It was he who was the leader of the church in Jerusalem. He was the one who brokered the compromise (Acts 15) that allowed Gentiles to join the early church.

#   #   #   #

MAURY'S MUSING—PRAYER

The Medivac helicopter chopped the air into noisy pieces as it flew over our house and settled in the grass. The chopper often lands on the football field across the street from the mobile home park where we live. It airlifts stroke, accident and other victims to a trauma center in Seattle.

Some of our neighbors and I walk to the street edge to watch the patient's transfer from the aid car to the aircraft. We have a high percentage of Christians here and I imagine some of them do what I do—pray silently for that victim.

Unless I have had my scanner radio on, I don't know the exact problem. Generally I pray that person has another chance to join the Kingdom of God if he/she isn't a citizen already. Often, I let the Lord sort out the specific need.

At times, I chauffeur Happy-Toes to the mall. While she is seeking out the items on her shopping list, I hobble to the food court. That is the place to watch people! If the passers-by don't have an apparent need, I pray for a blessing for them. Thus occupied, the time sure flies.

1 Thess. 5:17,18 Pray *without ceasing;*
in everything give thanks;
For this is God's will for you in Christ Jesus.

I don't think the Lord minds when I pause to enjoy a cup of Macdonald's coffee and a tasty, sweet Cinnabon. I surely give Him thanks for those goodies.

\#   \#   \#   \#

MAURY'S MUSING—ON TREASURES

The emcee said, "The lady paid $5 for this painting at a yard sale and it is expected to bring $17,000-$19,000 at an auction. It's a real treasure!

The next day, we were driving to the grocery store when Happy-Toes exclaimed, "there's one now, turn right!"

The signs led us to a garage sale. While HT went to inspect the merchandise, I drowsed, trying to figure out if I could handle $17,000. I awoke when HT opened the car door.

Instead of a magnificent painting by an old master, she had BABY CLOTHES!

"Not that, I'm 76 years old and we've already raised—."

Happy-Toes laughed, "they aren't for us silly, these are for missionaries, unwed mothers and poor folks in Appalachia."

Well, I'm glad and I never did figure out what I would do with $17,000 anyway.

> *"Do not lay up for yourselves treasures upon earth, where moth and rust destroy, and where thieves break in and steal But lay up for yourselves treasures in Heaven where neither moth nor rust destroys, and where thieves do not break in or steal; for where your treasure is, there will your heart be also."*
> Matt. 6:19-21.

*   *   *   *   *

Maurice (Maury) A. Johnson

MAURY'S MUSING—HEAVENLY PETS.

The elderly lady wanted to know if she could have her pet poodle in Heaven. Pets mean a lot to the older widows and widowers here in the senior mobile home park where Happy-Toes and I live. The dogs and cats are constant companions to their owners and in a lot of cases give these folks a reason to get up in the morning.

The pets, many of the four-legged animals and birds are neffish, or soulish creatures. That is, they relate to humans. In Isaiah, chapters 11 and 65, we see that animals will be present during the millenium. We can expect animals to be in Heaven also.

Personally, I like a good horse and when Jesus returns to earth at Armageddon, he will be riding a white horse (Rev. 19:11). I will be, too (Rev. 19:14).

Now, if that lady wants her poodle, I've got news for her. Psa. 37:4. *Delight yourself also in the Lord, and He will give you the desires of your heart.*

\#   \#   \#   \#

MAURY'S MUSING—ETs.

A few years ago, Hollywood discovered Extra-Terrestrial (ET) beings. They were about 3000 years behind the times. In fact, the off-spring of ETs called Nephilim (giants), were one of the reasons for the flood! But, let's tell it in the language of Genesis. Gen. 6:4. *The Nephilim were on the earth in those days, and also afterward, when the sons of God came in to the daughters of men, and they bore children to them. Those were the mighty men of old, men of renown.*

The "also afterwards'" refers to after the great flood. One of those ET offspring was the guy from Gath. The guy was 9 feet, 9 inches tall. His name, Goliath has come to mean something huge.

Goliath was a soldier of fortune for the Philistines. They believed they were unbeatable with the giant on their side. They didn't reckon with a little shepherd boy who had God on his side.

David chose five smooth stones from the creek for his sling ammunition. Four were for the giant's sons, if needed. When the first stone flew straight and true and buried itself in the forehead of Goliath, the rest of the Philistine army fled. The giant's sons were killed later (2 Sam.21:15-22).

I'm looking forward to a meeting with David in the millenium. He's scheduled to be King of Israel.

Who needs Hollywood?

#   #   #   #

MAURY'S MUSING—KING JAMES.

My parents dearly loved the King James (KJV) Bible but when I was a kid, the "thees and thous" threw me. I didn't understand a great deal of what I read.

When I got older and prayed for wisdom and understanding, I felt led to the New American Standard (NAS) version. For accuracy the NAS and the New International Version (NIV) are comparable. Until we started printing the Gospel and the lessons in the church program, the NAS was my carry-to-church Bible.

I do use other Bibles for clarification during study; the Greek Testament, the Jerusalem Bible and the Good News Bible as well as several study guides. I am sad, my NAS is wearing out despite being so careful with it. With that Bible, I can nearly open it to a passage I want. So many rich passages are highlighted and/or noted.

I do have a new Bible waiting in the wings and I am beginning to mark it up also. It is the New King James Version (NKJV). It is the same lyrical script that my parents loved but without the thees and thous.

King James the First hired the best interpreters and poets when he brought the KJV into being in 1611. In doing so, he put the English language Bible into the hands of the common folk. He gave a big boost to the printing industry for the Bible is the all-time world's best seller. He also gave the perfume industry a shot in the arm. You see, King James bragged that he never took a bath!

\#   \#   \#   \#

MAURY'S MUSING—IDENTIFICATION

"What in the world is this doing here," I asked. I was referring to one of our address labels that was stuck to the lapel of my jacket.

Happy-Toes laughed. "I used your jacket when I went for a walk in the sunshine yesterday. I stuck that label on in case I should keel over on my walk so whoever finds me will know where I came from. Clever, huh?"

Both HT and I have had a number of serious illnesses and it is possible that we could collapse from some of them. We men generally carry wallets with identification in them, but HT doesn't have her ID when she walks. Neither of us have any fears about leaving this scene in God's time.

Whether we know it or not, we do have ID if we belong to the Lord. Remember that cross the pastor that baptized you marked on your forehead? It doesn't have to be tattooed on. There is another ID that children of God don't want. I won't be there, but during the Tribulation period, if you are still around, the antichrist will make you take his ID to do business.

Rev. 13:16,17 *And he causes all, the small and the great, and the rich and the poor, and the free men and the slaves, to be given a mark on their Right hand, or on their forehead, and he provides that no one should be able to buy or sell, except the one who has the mark, either the name of the beast or the number of his name.*

#   #   #   #

Maurice (Maury) A. Johnson

MAURY'S MUSING—SIX DAYS.

"Our Creator might have made the universe in six 24-hour days and made it look older," said my friend.

"No," said I, "God is absolute truth and to Him that deception would be a lie."

We had been discussing the days of creation. The word *yom* is the Hebrew word which we interpret as day. Yom, however, can mean differing indefinite time periods as well. The latest scientific discoveries show that the Bibical order of creation is correct, but the yoms are thousands of years longer than 24 hours. The Bible gives us examples of longer-than-24 hour-days.

We know that the Creator is still on the day of rest from creating. He has been on that 7th yom for about 6000 years. Then too, we have no idea of how long the day of the Lord or the day of salvation might be. Of course, time means nothing to One who has no beginning and no end.

> *But do not let this one fact escape your notice, beloved, that with the Lord one day is as a thousand years, and a thousand years as one day. (2 Peter 3:8)*

No, the Bible and science cannot disagree for God created both.

# # # #

MAURY'S MUSING—VICTORY ROLL

The victory roll was a thing of beauty. The red-tailed P-38 Lightning gleamed in the sun as it slow-rolled across the blue sky above our olive-drab tent homes.

As our bombing missions became longer, stretching into Austria and Germany from our base in Southern Italy, we flew every-other day. We didn't have pressurized cabins and so the high altitude temperatures of 20-50 below coupled with our breathing in oxygen masks for eight to eleven hours at a time nearly exhausted us. Thus, half of our combat crews would fly each day. On our "off" day, we would train new crews or transport personnel around the Mediterranean.

Those of us who were "off" awaited word of the day's mission but radio silence was strictly enforced. Two of our fighter escort planes which were based in Northern Italy would come down and give us the victory roll sign if the mission was a success.

According to my study of Bible prophesy, there is a rapture in our future. It is the time when we who are redeemed will defy gravity and rise to meet our Lord in the clouds.

> 1 Thess. 4:16b-17: *And the dead in Christ will rise first. Then We who are alive and remain shall be caught up together with Them in the clouds to meet the Lord in the air.*

Maurice (Maury) A. Johnson

I wonder if the Lord would mind if I did some victory rolls on my way up? Not for me! For Him and His successful mission here on earth.

\#   \#   \#   \#

MAURY'S MUSING—REWARD

The cry for help came from the direction of the bog. Farmer Fleming, a poor Scot, dropped his tools and ran to the swamp. There, mired to the waist and struggling in vain to free himself and reach dry land, was a boy. Fleming saved the lad from a slow terrifying death in that peat bog.

The following day an elegant carriage pulled up to the Scotsman's meager home. A finely-dressed gentleman stepped out and introduced himself to the farmer.

"I am the father of the lad you saved," he said," and I would like to give you a reward."

"Nae," said the Scot, "I want no reward."

"Is that your son," he asked about the boy standing nearby.

"Yes," he said proudly.

"Let me take him and give him a good education, then. If he is like his father, he'll grow to be a man you can be proud of."

Years later, the farmer's son graduated from St. Mary's Hospital Medical School in London. Later, he became Sir Arthur Fleming, the man who discovered penicillin. When the nobleman's son contacted pneumonia, it was penicillin that saved his life.

The nobleman? His name was Randolph Churchill. His son became Sir Winston Churchill, the man who saved England during World War 2.

The Lord works in mysterious ways, His wonders to perform.

#   #   #   #

MAURY'S MUSING—FOOTPRINTS

"That is a different pin you are wearing," I said to Happy-Toes. The silver pin was shaped like two perfect miniature footprints.

"Those footprints are the size of those of a ten-week old unborn baby in it's mother's womb," said HT, "My friend Anitia gave me the pin."

I looked at my size eleven and a half feet then back to those tiny footprints and I wondered. Are we cheating ourselves of something wonderful? Setting aside the bibical view, I pondered.

The latest guess-timate of abortions performed since Roe v. Wade that I have seen is 10,000,000. If we can agree that one out of 1,000 people are great achievers, that is 10,000 super people we have lost. Oh, how we could use 10,000 poets that stir the soul; doctors who could find cures for cancer and AIDS; evangelists to convict us of sin; statesmen to bring us peace and musicians to calm our inner being.

We know that Jeremiah was called when he was yet unborn.

> *"Before I formed you in the womb I knew you;*
> *Before you were Born I sanctified you; I*
> *ordained you a prophet to the nations."*
> Jeremiah 1:5

#   #   #   #

MAURY'S MUSING—ANGER.

"Boy, he was mad," said Happy-Toes.

We had just watched a news replay that showed a basketball player giving a member of the opposing team a knuckle sandwich. A coach that jumped in the middle of the players collected a row of stitches for his trouble. HT and I enjoy boxing matches but we don't expect to see one during during a round ball game.

"Yeah, even God gets mad sometimes" I said.

We don't hear about God's anger much anymore. Our soul-saving nowadays stresses His wondrous love, but He has another side, too. When I was a kid, preachers didn't hesitate when it came to telling about hells fire. Billy Sunday, the baseball player turned evangelist, used the Lake of Fire as a tool to save many souls.

We are told that God is slow to anger (Nahum 1:3), but He does get angry! Remember the cities of the plain? He got real mad and destroyed Sodom and Gomorrah and the other cities for their immoral behavior.

And don't forget the cities of Sodom and Gomorrah and their neighboring Towns, all full of lust of every kind including lust of men for other men. These cities were destroyed by fire and continue to be a warning to us that there is a hell in which sinners are punished. (Jude 1:7)

The last half of the seven-year tribulation is called the Great Tribulation. It features God's anger in a big way

279

during this last chance for those who hadn't accepted His gift of salvation.   For those of us who have this is our promise:

> *And since by His blood He did all this for us as sinners, how Much will He do for us now that He has declared us not guilty?   Now He will save us from all of God's wrath to come. (Romans 5:9).*

#   #   #   #

MAURY'S MUSING—COLUMBUS

"They sure want to talk bad about good people," said Happy-Toes. "They must have terrible hearts!"

We were discussing how revisionists make up bad things about people long dead. They trash good folks like George Washington, Abraham Lincoln and Christopher Columbus. These are fine people that God sent to us at the proper time in history. I guess those revisionists never read Philippians 4:8.

They revile Christopher Columbus and say that he was responsible for bringing disease and destroying the peace and tranquility of the New World. I've got news for them!

First, the Garden of Eden was not in America and secondly, sin got here before Chris did. On a subsequent trip here, he found natives roasting human body parts over a bonfire and the crew brought home as many diseases as they left.

On October 12, we celebrate the accomplishments of a fine Christian man, Christopher Columbus. His was a missionary zeal to find a short way to the Orient to bring them the good news of Jesus Christ. While the rest of the world thought that the earth was flat, either he or his uncle, a noted Bible scholar, must have read Isaiah 40:22.

It is He who sits above the circle of the earth,
And it's inhabitants are like grasshoppers,
Who stretches out the heavens like a curtain,
And spreads them out like a tent to dwell in.

\#   \#   \#   \#

281

Maurice (Maury) A. Johnson

——A NEW EARTH

After Armageddon, when Jesus destroys the great armies of the world near Jerusalem, a period of 1,000 years (millennium) of peace and prosperity will follow. Armageddon is the last hurrah for anything military. From that time on, all efforts will focus on positive things.

We, the Christians, will be joined by the Old Testament Saints and those saints who were martyred during the tribulation. We will all be in our new indestructible bodies. At the same time, people who survived the tribulation will be present on earth in their old natural bodies. They will have an opportunity to become believers in the best of times.

After a last rebellion, near the end of the millennium, we see the last of the natural-bodied people. Some will join the saints and some will go to judgement with Satan.

By this time, the world has seen a lot of sin and wear and tear. The events of the tribulation alone have taken a great toll. Earthquakes have created great fissures in the earth's crust, sunk islands and leveled mountains. Weapons of war have fouled the air and water. Sin, too has left it's mark on terra firma. It's signs are everywhere. Much as archeologists of our time dig up idols of worship, vestiges of old ways remain.

Talk about housecleaning! God, who felt remorse when He destroyed the earth with water, will do it with fire this time. (2 Peter 3:11-13) Don't worry, God has a plan for us.

"Loom I am creating new heavens and a new earth—so wonderful that no one will even think

282

about the old ones anymore.   Be glad; rejoice forever in My creation!" (Isa. 65:17,18a)

\#   \#   \#   \#

Maurice (Maury) A. Johnson

MAURY'S MUSING—HOME

"It had to be 1930 or earlier," said Happy-Toes. "It was before my sister and I went to school."

HT's mother was the organist at Our Savior's Lutheran Church in Bremerton, Washington for 38 years and HT was telling how she first remembered Poulsbo, a small town some 10 miles away, where we now live. Her mother accompanied their pastor Sunday night to play for services at the Children's Home and Happy-Toes and her sister came along.

The Children's Home was a project of local Lutherans. It provided a home for orphan boys as well as keeping those whose parents were in dire straits because of a terrible depression that was in full bloom.

The home was on land farmed by the child residents and provided much of the needed food. Some of the people raised there have great things to say about their time at the home.

That boys home expanded into a large complex and became Martha and Mary, The Home of Loving Kindness. It now has a children's day care, a Christian kindergarten, a seniors apartment house (Ebenezer) and a 170-bed nursing home facility with wings for Alzheimer patients and those needing physical therapy. The old orphan's home is long gone but the nursing home covers the area.

Happy-Toes' mom lived in those Ebenezer Apartments for seven years. She spent the last five days of her life on earth at Martha and Mary Nursing Home. Then, she was transported to Heaven. By my calculations and memory, she left us nearly on the exact same spot where she played the organ at worship seventy years before.

#   #   #   #

Maurice (Maury) A. Johnson

MAURY'S MUSING—LOAVES AND FISHES

"Why don't you stay and have dinner with us," said the voice of Happy-Toes in the kitchen.

I figured #1 daughter had stopped by after work and I went back to working on my computer. A short time later, I heard:

"Why don't you stay and have dinner with us."

Could it be that we have a delayed echo in our mobile home? I wandered into the kitchen to satisfy my curiosity. Number two bachelor grandson had stopped by after work to have coffee with us and a fourth plate was added to the table.

Two more grandsons popped in after swim team practice and I held my breath. As I do a lot of our grocery shopping, I knew we had two very small skirt steaks for dinner. The two latest grandson visitors were headed someplace else for hamburgers and just came by to say "hi."

Happy-Toes found another piece of meat in the freezer to zap and she always does extra spuds and veggies. Drop-in company at meal time never fazes HT. She glories in it. One of her gifts is the gift of hospitality.

Maybe I'm learning from her. I did sloppy-joes, potato salad and peach crisp the night before and I had enough for one extra grand-kid who happened by.

Counting spouses, we have 26 people in our very close family and, no, I am not the patriarch. That job belongs to our Father God!

He predestined us to adoption as sons through Jesus Christ to Himself, according to the kind intention of His will Ephesians 1:5.

Maurice (Maury) A. Johnson

MAURY'S MUSING—MILLENNIUM.

Much ado has been made about turning over a calendar leaf and finding the year 2000 or 2 001 bringing us into a new millennium. Happy-Toes and I have relatives that would not fly on January 1, 2000, lest the flight computers turn to Jello on that date.

I've known of several people that are still eating dehydrated beans and drinking bottled water they had hoarded for that big event in case a catastrophe were to follow. Many folks made a big fuss when the year 1000 came along, also.

Barnabas thought that this particular millennium of ours was special. You remember Barnabas, he was a fellow missionary with Paul. He was also the uncle of John Mark, the author of the second gospel. Here is what he said.

And God made in six days the works of his hands; and He finished them on the seventh day, and He rested on the seventh day and sanctified it. Consider my children, what that signifies. He finished them in six days. The meaning of it is this; that in six thousand years the Lord will bring all things to an end. For with Him one day is as a thousand years, as Himself testifieth, saying, Behold, this day shall be as a thousand years. Therefore children, in six days, that is, in six thousand years, shall all things be accomplished. And what is that He saith. And He rested the seventh day; He meaneth this: that when His Son shall come, and abolish the season of the wicked one, and judge the ungodly, and shall change the sun and the moon and the stars; then He shall gloriously rest in that seventh day.

The Lord does equate a thousand years with a day. (2 Peter 3:8, Psa. 90:4) The tables of generations would seem to put Adam and the flood 2000 years apart. From the flood to Jesus was about another 2000 and 2000 more years to our time. If Barnabas is right, I've got some variables for him. Various historians place Jesus' birthday in 02, 03 or 04 A.D. Then, there is some slop in the changing of calendars from Hebrew to the Gregorian to the Julian.

Let's all be ready for our rapture ALL the time like the Lord tells us! Come Lord Jesus!

#   #   #   #

Maurice (Maury) A. Johnson

MAURY'S MUSING—SHOE BOXES

"It is, it is, that's my shoebox," yelled Happy-Toes with a big smile!

Our #1 daughter had brought us a brochure on Samaritan's Purse featuring Operation Christmas Child. There on page 2 was a picture of a shoebox and it's contents. It was the collection that HT had lovingly assembled for some child last Christmas season.

Some years ago, Franklin, the son of Billy Graham, founded the ministry, Samaritan's Purse. The ministry focuses on bringing Christ to the world's trouble spots. One of the ways is the shoebox ministry, a program to give toys to children of poverty all over the world. With the toys comes the good news of Jesus.

Happy-Toes and I were born during a great depression and didn't have many toys ourselves. Some years ago, one of our kids got us started with this fun program. Now, our congregation's Sunday School has gotten into the act.

HT covers our boxes with pretty Christmas paper. Then, the fun begins! She shops for a girl about 5-10 years old and I pick gifts for a boy.

Last Christmas, more than 4 million boxes were given. They came from Australia, Canada, Finland, Germany, Ireland, Netherlands, the United Kingdom and the United States.

"Samaritan's Purse is doing a great thing here, putting a smile on those kid's faces—you can't buy that with money." Sammy Sosa, major league baseball star and Operation Christmas Child participant.

I can hardly wait. I think I'll get an early start on my shoebox this year.

# # # #

MAURY'S MUSING—NEANDERTHALS

"Is our favorite program on tonight," asked Happy-Toes?

I consulted the TV section of our local newspaper and answered. "Yes, the Forensic Detectives is scheduled at nine."

The program features actual murder cases and how they were solved using scientific methods. Many of the cases were solved using deoxyribonucleic acid genetic markers. Now you know why we just call it DNA. Like fingerprints, DNA has a different pattern for each individual. It is a life protein which is found in every cell in our bodies. Our Creator, who dislikes clones, gave us DNA to make sure that we would all be different in dimensions, features and coloration. Through DNA testing, relationships can be determined and family lines can be found.

Since the discovery of bones of Neanderthal Man, evolutionists and other pseudo-intellectuals have declared him to be the immediate ancestor to mankind. The Neanderthals walked erect and lived between 150,000 and 30,000 years ago.

Recently, two independent studies made by researchers at the Universities of Stockholm and Glasgow have tossed a monkey wrench into the thinking of evolutionists. First, researchers painstakingly drew DNA from a Neanderthal skeleton about 70,000 years old and then from an infant one about 29,000 years old. Both research teams reported the same results. Neanderthals made no contribution to the genetics of modern man!

Shucks, we Christians knew that!

Genesis 2:7 *And the Lord God formed man*
Of the dust of the ground and breathed
Into his nostrils the breath of life; and
man became a living being.

Maurice (Maury) A. Johnson

MAURY'S MUSING—DECEPTION

Excellent, very satisfying, I thought as I placed my napkin on the table. Happy-Toes smiled as she was congratulated by the two couples we had entertained. HT has the gift of hospitality, but she didn't always know it.

My mind took me back to 1942. I had just graduated from high school and being too young to enter the service, I went to work in the shipyard temporarily. There I met Happy-Toes. She was a high school junior. As part of the all-out effort during World War Two, the local high school kids went to school for four hours and worked for eight. HT and I made the magnificent wage of $50 a month.

When I first saw this little chickie, I did a head-over-heels tumble and never did recover. Toward the beginning of our two-year courtship, she invited me to dinner at her parent's place on one of our very rare days off.

I don't remember what we had, but I do recall that everything was excellent. I imagine that the meal blew a months allotment of food ration stamps. It was years later, long after I returned from the air war in Europe that I found out the truth. HT's younger sister had prepared that meal. I have since forgiven HT and her sister is one of my favorite people. HT didn't mean to deceive me, but she let me assume that she had done the cooking.

Deception is a tactic used by Satan. He likes to get our heads nodding up and down and then slip one past us. Jesus warns us about false teachers in the last days, even in the church. As best as I can tell, there are 230 people now who claim to be the Messiah plus a whole lot of teachers who would give us bum dope.

294

"For false christs and false prophets will rise and show great signs And wonders to deceive, if possible, even the elect. Matt. 24:24.

\#   \#   \#   \#

———HORSES

Happy-Toes and I enjoy horses. We like to watch equestrian events and rodeo on television as well as the hunter/jumper events a granddaughter competes in. She is an excellent rider and sits her thoroughbred, Reggie, very well.

Five generations earlier, my grandad, came West in a horse-drawn wagon. He was a big for his age, 12-year-old, and he drove the third wagon for two families on the trek. The family income was derived from horses. He and his father captured wild horses that descended from the animals the Spanish explorers left. They were abundant in the great basins and plains of Montana.

George Lee, my grandfather, green-broke the critters, took them back East and sold them. He had a way with all animals that was passed down to our granddaughter. Later, he drove stagecoach to gold mine towns in the Helena area.

I'm glad we will have animals during the 1,000 years following the tribulation. Cows, bears, lions and cobras are mentioned but they will eat grass. It appears that God's chosen people will be farmers and will appreciate horseflesh.

> *On that day even the harness bells of the horses will be inscribed with these words: Set Apart as Holy to the Lord. (Zech. 14:20)*

\#   \#   \#   \#

———THE NUMBERS GAME

"One forty-three," I said. Happy-Toes smiled as she crowed, "one-seventeen."

HT and I both have Diabetes and we have to test our blood sugar twice a day. We prick our fingers with medical needles and submit a sample to an automated computer-type instrument. That tool gives a readout. The amount of blood sugar on that readout gives an indication of how much insulin or medication we need. This morning we were both well within the allowable limits.

There is also danger in not having enough sugar. This could cause a diabetic coma and worse. One day, my wife Happy-Toes and I, had been shopping all morning. We hadn't taken time to rest or snack and HT felt she was getting faint. I stopped at a Dairy Queen and helped her in. After a grease burger, fries and ice cream she started to come around. Now, I keep sucrose pills in her purse and in the car for emergencies.

Type 2 diabetes is the kind you get when you are older. I guess I got it because I outlived my pancreas, the gland that handles body sugar. Once considered an old folks disease, Type 2 diabetes is now effecting people at a younger age.

I told Doctor Bruce about the lousy circulation in my legs and feet and also mentioned that I was having a tough time reading the funny papers. He thought that was serious and tested me for diabetes.

Not taking precautions with diabetes can result in blindness or foot/leg amputations. Sixteen million people in the U.S. have the disease, but five million of them don't know it.

#   #   #   #

———IDENTIFICATION

The nurse, that told me about my diabetes, strongly suggested that I get a visible medic-alerting-type ID to warn of my condition. In the packet I received when diagnosed with diabetes, was literature telling about dog-tag type IDs. I ordered bracelets for both Happy-Toes, who also has diabetes, and me.

With this ailment it is possible to pass out from either too much or not enough sugar. If I should hit the pavement, the people who come to my aid have a clue as to why.

The bracelet had room for three short lines to be engraved on it so I had to settle on a message. I didn't think that my asbestosis, bad back, psoriasis, arthritis or hem—er minor ailments would be earth-shaking enough to advertize on my wrist. I settled for my heart problem, diabetes and a major allergy. I would like to have added, "citizen of Heaven to be."

God and Satan both like to use identification marks. After we are gone in the rapture, 144,000 Jews will realize Jesus is the Messiah. They will receive God's ID.

And I heard how many were marked with the seal of God. There were 144, 000 who were sealed from the tribes of Israel (Rev. 7:4)

Satan's ID spells doom for anyone who takes it. A Florida firm markets a computer chip that is a combination ID/health record that is implanted under a person's skin. This could well be Satan's tool.

Maurice (Maury) A. Johnson

He required everyone-great and small, rich and poor, slave and free-to be given a mark on the right hand or on the forehead. And no one could buy or sell anything without that mark, which was either the name of the beast or the number representing his name. (Rev. 13:16,17)

\# \# \# \#

MAURY'S MUSING—BREAD

"The daycare notation said that Lucas, our one-year-old great-grandson, ate all his lunch. Two wieners, one jar of applesauce and his taco." Happy-Toes laughed.

Actually, the bread Lukey ate was lefse, a Norwegian flatbread. Every ethnic group has a form of flat or fried bread. Lefse is made from potatoes while the Mexican tortilla is generally made from corn. Happy-Toes always makes extra smashed spuds so she can turn them into lefse after supper. Her excuse for the extra potatoes is always that Anitia, or Angie, or George, or Edie, or Phyllis, or _____ likes lefse. I have tried to tell her that it is not a miracle food to no avail.

In Jesus' day, the Hebrew flatbread was plate, spoon and napkin. Let's look in as a family from a lower economic class has dinner.

The family is sitting on mats in a circle. In the center of the circle are clay pots containing beans or lentils while greens could be chard or mustard. Onions, too were common. Food, unlike clothing, was inexpensive. The family members would use the flat bread as a spoon to scoop up and eat the vittles. Don't look for meat! It was only served on festive occasions. Even on Sabbaths only well-to-do people would have meat. Bread scraps would be used to clean fingers as we use napkins. Perhaps these were the scraps that fell from the table in Luke 16:21.

It's fitting that our Lord used bread to commune with us, His adopted sons and daughters.

Maurice (Maury) A. Johnson

"I am the living bread which came down from heaven. If anyone eats of this bread, he will live forever; and the bread that I shall give is My flesh, which I shall give for The life of the world" John 6:51

#   #   #   #

MAURY'S MUSING—GENEROSITY

"I've been keeping track on the calendar and it's time to change flags," said Happy-Toes.

It has been my custom to erect a flagpole at each place that we've owned. This last time I didn't get one from the woods. I bought a nice telescoping aluminum pole. It's 20 feet tall and has hardware to fly two flags at once. The top flag is "Old Glory" of course, a symbol of this country where we can worship God as we see fit. I fought a bloody war to make sure of that.

Then comes the stickler, flag #2. I'm half Swedish and I enjoy flying that blue and yellow banner, Last Christmas I bought Happy-Toes a Norwegian flag and I offered to fly it every fifth Tuesday. I think she has been studying new math. She wants me to fly that one 3/4s of the time because she is 75% Norske.

I read her Ephesians 5:22-24:

> *Wives, submit to your own husbands, as to the Lord. For The husband is head of the wife, as also Christ is head of The Church; and He is the Savior of the body. Therefore, just as the church is subject to Christ, so let the wives be to Their own husbands in everything.*

Happy-Toes says she loves me. Aw, what's a little air time for flags, anyway?

# # # #

Maurice (Maury) A. Johnson

Heavenly Days

But no heavenly nights

Maurice (Maury) A. Johnson

────HEAVENLY DAYS

"Heavenly days, McGee," was the favorite saying of the distaff half of the radio comedy team, Fibber McGee and Molly. We are sure that the days with our Lord will be heavenly but don't expect to see heavenly nights!

What do we know about Heaven? The Bible just seems to give enough information to whet the appetites of those of us who are older or have accumulated a passel of aches and pains. Well, through exegesis, we know more than we think we know! For one thing, we know what <u>won't</u> be there.

When I was young and starting to raise a family, it seems our family car was always old. The tires and the battery were forever tired and I hoped for better days when those items would be less troublesome. Now that we have a car that is only a half-dozen years old, and I can afford to keep it up, my 75-year-old-body has seen better days. When the Lord calls me home, I'll be happy to trade it in.

Besides, I'm already dead—to sin that is! Through baptism, I participated in our Lord's crucifixion and His resurrection also! (Romans 6:5) My friend, Ben, reminds me the 23rd Psalm says that when I leave my body behind, I'll just experience the SHADOW of death.

When we take our last breath, our decision as to our destination has already been made. There is no changing our ticket. For you, my brothers and sisters of the Roman Catholic faith, my Bible does not tell of a half-way place. No purgatory, it's just Heaven or Hell.

Well, back to Heaven and what we can expect. When my body dies, I will go to Heaven in recognizable spirit form. The Lord already has built a fine house for me. (John 14:2) If I should still be around when the Lord calls all the saints home via the rapture, we will get new indestructible bodies on the way up. (1 Thess. 4:15-18)

We will know and we will be known. First things first! I will kneel before our Savior and thank Him. Then, after a joyous reunion with my parents, grandparents and in-laws, I expect to recognize all the saints and patriarchs. They, in turn, will know me. In all probability, we won't need name tags. (1 Cor. 13:12)

I mentioned earlier about nights. There is no darkness in Heaven! God is light! Probably one of the first things we will notice is that there are no shadows. You see, shadows require some darkness. (1 John 1:5) (Rev. 22:5)

One of the jobs I had as a young man was in a lumberyard/hardware store. It was a joy to wait on people and help solve their problems. Jesus' ministry here on earth was spent in service to others. He exhorted us to feed,— visit,—help! We can expect to serve and be served. Waitresses and barbers should have a head start in Heaven. (Matt. 20:25-28)

Happy-Toes and I often remark how wonderful it is that we can enjoy fruit for so much of the year. It wasn't too long ago that the availability of peaches or watermelon was restricted to a local season. Folks, I enjoy eating! I'm real glad that our Lord had an appetite after his resurrection. (John 21:10) Those 12 fruit trees that are along the river of life sound good to me! (Rev. 22:2) The wedding feast as we become the Bride of Christ after the rapture promises to be a dandy. (Rev. 19:7-10)

Down here, the price of medical insurance has skyrocketed the last few years. That will not be a concern to us. My back and leg pains will be all gone. (Rev. 21:4) I imagine John, the recipient of the Revelation, who was believed to be near 90 when the Lord showed him all this probably had arthritis, too. He had been sleeping on that cold dungeon floor on the Isle of Patmos which wouldn't help matters. He's in Heaven now, and his pains are history.

Remember the curse God put on the earth when Adam and Eve sinned? (Gen. 3:14-19) Kaput, all gone! Goodbye to thorns, thistles, weeds and poison ivy! Without a need to populate Heaven, we don't have to fret about the pain of childbirth. (Rev. 22:3) We will be neuters, anyway. (Gal. 3:28) (Mark 12:25) (Luke 20;34-36} The sexual process that has caused so much sin here on earth will be no more. Don't worry, our Lord has prepared delights that far outshine our earthly ones. (2 Cor. 4:15-17)

I had flown to the Hawaiian Islands several times as a member of the Naval Air Reserve. I had enjoyed the Island experience and when I was able, I took Happy-Toes to Oahu to share the joy. As we left the aircraft in Honolulu it hit us, the smell of many, many flowers. How wonderful! Some of our garden "musts" are sweet peas with their beautiful smell and Happy-Toes keeps bowls of them in our house all summer. Floral scents and blossoms are a creation of our Creator, expect to enjoy them forever!

For all you ladies of fashion, the latest news is— beautiful white linen! For all the fashion designers that have been pushing unisex garments, enjoy, but you had better develop new skills if you are believers. Clothe designers won't be needed.

HT and I live in an area that is loaded with scenery. Much of the year we can snow ski and within two hours we can be water skiing on either fresh or salt water. Sometimes, on a winter morning, I scarce can catch my breath as I view the snow-capped peaks. Our Creator gave us first-class scenery. The things He made for our enjoyment here on earth are not second class! Let's look for more of the same, there.

God does not have to have a learning curve! He doesn't have to make an amoeba before He makes a housefly before He makes a monkey. He made a first-class earth, the only thing that loused it up was sin. Expect to see mountains, beautiful waterfalls and gorgeous forests. He is all knowing and all powerful!

I have what is known as a tin ear. I couldn't carry a tune in an 18-wheeler. This is probably related to my deafness, but I love to listen to music. I have to believe Heaven will be full of it. King David will be there and he is a fine musician. It doesn't say how big his choir was, but he had a 4000 piece band, back then. All you people with lovely voices and instrumental talents will have a niche. I even expect to sound much better there.

Don't expect to be sitting around on a cloud playing a harp all day! Our first priority will be to worship our wonderful God. When we come back with our Lord at Armageddon, we will rule and reign with Him. Who will we rule? (Rev. 20:6) The millions of people who are still in their natural bodies who survived at the second coming of the Lord. These people will need governors, mayors, judges etal. Jesus is King of Kings and Lord of Lords. (1 Tim. 6:15) The chain of command for Israel is given to us. King David is King (2 Sam. 7:16) and the disciples each are over one of the 12 tribes. (Luke 22:30)

Science tells us that we use very little of our God-given brain. Only people like Albert Einstein or Steven Hawking even attain a 10% use of their gray matter. The reason, of course, is that we have stored useless garbage in it. We have stored junk from movies, TV, books, newspapers and other sources up there. In Heaven, all that useless trivia will be gone and we'll have 100% brain usage as God intended.

What will we do with all that brainpower and time? Here on earth, after that terrible seven year tribulation period, we'll have an awful mess to clean up. With much of the water sources lifeless, forests burnt and pollution from nuclear and biological weapons, there will be an immense cleanup necessary. Our Creator will create again when He finishes His day of rest, and we will help Him!

One of the ways we will know each other is by character and personality. The same character and personality we have made on earth! Are you loving?—happy—generous?

Earlier, I mentioned what won't be in Heaven. Nothing will be there that DEFILES! (Rev. 21:27) What does defile mean? Webster says; to make dirty, or unclean. It also means to pollute, desecrate or profane. That is one reason we know that our sanctification will be complete when we enter those pearly gates! We will have no inclination to sin!

Here on earth we have laws that govern our existence and are necessary for life. One is gravity. We would all fly off into space without it. Our vascular systems wouldn't work without gravity. Another one is the Second Law of Thermodynamics and one of it's components, entropy. One of entropy's jobs is to defile so that life here is possible. But, it won't be a law in Heaven! With entropy, iron and other metals rust and return to the soil. Plants and animals die and do the same. Mountains become stones, then sand, then soil. Animal and human wastes replenish the soil. If we didn't have entropy, the defiler, we would be atop several thousand feet of dead bodies and unrotted garbage trying to raise carrots. As our God creates again, expect not to see garbage cans, compost piles or bathrooms!

With entropy, everything gets worse not better, so entropy is one of the reasons evolutionary beginnings are not possible. If we were to set a new Rolls Royce in a field and leave it for a few years, it would turn into a pile of rust. If evolutionary beginnings were the rule, we could put a pile of rust in that pasture and it would become a new Rolls!

As an old war horse, I was once commissioned as a Colonel in the Confederate Air Force. I did fight in World War 2 and was prepared to defend my country for another 20 years. Military titles will mean nothing when we get to Heaven. I will be Saint Maury. (Isaiah 2:4)

I once read a dissertation by a theologian who figured that Heaven was a spirit world which existed in the same place that we in the world occupy. Not so! Isaiah tells us that Satan believes he can usurp the throne of God which is above the stars, in the North. (Isa. 13:14) In fact, the word, "Heaven", means heights or great heights! When Paul visited Heaven, he called it the third Heaven. (2 Cor. 12:2) The first is the earth's troposphere, the second is out where our spaceships check on Mars and Pluto. The third, then is way out. (Eph. 4:10)

The other destination for earth folks is down, we are told in Genesis and Ephesians. (**Eph.** 4:9) In Job, we read that it is under the sea and it's inhabitants. (Job 26:5) Peter tells about Hell being pits of darkness. (2 Peter 2:4) Anyway, Hell is just the holding area until the judgement day when the folks imprisoned there will be banished to the Lake of Fire, forever. (Rev. 21:8)

I have made my choice. I hope you have chosen Heaven, too. I expect to be totally awed by the Glory of God. (1 Cor. *2:9)"But it is written: Eye has not seen, nor ear heard, nor have entered into the heart of man the things which God has prepared for those who love Him."*

—For thine is the Kingdom,—the Power,—and the Glory, for ever and ever, amen!

#   #   #   #

Maurice (Maury) A. Johnson

The Seven Churches

Through the ages

Maurice (Maury) A. Johnson

————THE CHURCHES

The mainline churches are under attack as Satan is having a last attempt to destroy them. As one who has studied prophesy for 40 years, I can clearly see the end of the age rushing at us. Lately, the Lord has been bringing my studies back again and again to the seven churches of Revelation. I'd better heed Him.

Until very recently, we couldn't understand what the Word of God tells us about the days to come. We're told that great increases in technology, knowledge and transportation are necessary before we could. (Dan. 12:4) Augustine and Luther, in their days, didn't have a chance of understanding the future. Most seminaries avoid the study with a purple passion and as a consequence nearly all pastors and Christians are completely ignorant of the subject. The study of end-times prophesy is called eschatology.

In the second and third chapters of Revelation, Jesus points out to John, and to us, seven churches that symbolize the Church through the ages and the church today. Only two of the seven pass muster with the Lord. Perhaps, you can find your church here.

EPHESUS: The Apostolic church. The Ephesian church is symbolic of the first century Church (A.D. 30-100). It was characterized by fervent evangelism. Some scriptural evidence seems to indicate that the gospel was preached around the world at this time. Another plus for this church was hatred for the Nicolaitans. (More later on this)

The downside was that apostate teachers infiltrated the church and were allowed to stay. The church had no written scriptures and it was fairly easy for false teachers to deceive. One problem was that "ecumania" was allowed. (One world church regardless of faith) Church discipline wasn't used to cleanse the rolls from heretics. Paul had warned about the heretics at Ephesus. (Acts 20:29-31) The church had lost it's first love, Jesus.

SMYRNA: The persecuted church. This one represents the church from A.D. 100-312. This covered the era when Paul was beheaded, Peter was crucified and Justin Martyr was killed. Under ten Roman emperors, Christians were boiled in oil, burned at the stake and fed alive to wild dogs, lions and bears. Scriptures were gathered and burned. One church historian places the number of martyred at near five million. Despite such adversity, the church grew and was faithful to Jesus Christ. Our Lord had nothing negative to say about the church at Smyrna. We can't say that about the next one!

PERGAMUM: The indulged church, A.D. 312-606. Pergamum was the capitol of Asia. It was also Satan's headquarters. The emperor of Rome, Constantine, gave the church government sanction and Christianity became the first state church. During this time, the church became worldly and doctrinal practices like these were introduced:

AD 300- Prayers for the dead.
AD 300- Making the sign of the cross.
AD 375- Worship of saints and angels.
AD 394- Mass instituted

318

AD 431- Worship of Mary begun.
AD 500- Priests began dressing differently than laymen.
AD 526- Extreme unction.
AD 593- Purgatory introduced.
AD 600- Services conducted in Latin.
AD 600- Prayers directed to Mary.

The doctrine of the Nicolaitans gained a foothold. This doctrine, taught by Nicolai, separated body and spirit, gave them license to sin with the body. Likewise, the spirit of Balaam allowed sexual sins and an unholy mixture of church and the world.

THYATIRA: The pagan church. AD 606 to the tribulation, it covers the Dark Ages. The light of this church nearly went out as it continued the practices of the preceding church and adopted more doctrinal changes.

AD 709- Kissing the popes foot.
AD 786- Worshiping of images and relics.
AD 850- Use of "holy water" begun.
AD 995- Canonization of dead saints.
AD 998- Fasting on Fridays and during lent.

The list goes on and on, and the light of this church was saved by the reformation. A mistake by Luther was to seek approval of the government. In all cases, state churches tend to make the populace believe they are automatically saved. We know that Christianity is an individual's decision. The reformation did not change much of the superfluous add-ons the church had collected over the years, either. Doctor Luther wanted to retain the one true church with a corrected doctrine.

SARDIS: The dead church, AD 1520 until the tribulation. This church will continue into the tribulation while the real believers have been taken to Heaven in the rapture. Some individuals from this church will overcome. See my note on the Laodicean church.

I have relatives in Sweden that say that Swedes go to church four times in their life. W__hen they are baptized, confirmed, married and buried. Friends in Norway say that, too. These are state churches. I think these are beyond saving, even with CPR! There, I've alienated some more friends.

PHILADELPHIA: The church Christ loves, AD 1750 to the rapture. Most of the churches turn me into a Gloomy Gus. Not so this one nor Smyrna.

It appears to me that three things make a church successful. A solid grasp of the scriptures and the teaching of them in a true fashion. An enthusiastic evangelism program and an exciting missionary outreach. We are witnessing tremendous growth in many congregations today who follow this blueprint. Philadelphia means brotherly love.

LAODICEA: The apostate church, 1900 into the tribulation. Did you ever expect a steaming hot mug of restaurant coffee only to sip lukewarm mud? That's how the Lord felt about this church, a successor to Pergamum.

Here we see a church in a rich area. Opulent members having tastes for beautiful buildings with lovely appointments, but no taste for the gospel.

Well, we have run the gamut of churches. We've seen rich ones that fail to do their duty, and persecuted churches that excel. Despite apostate leaders in the hierarchy of many churches, some individual congregations retain their "first love." Despite how bad the churches become, some individuals are "overcomers." These people know the Lord and they are meers of the Church of Jesus Christ.

Well, I found my long-time church here in Revelation and I am very disappointed with it. My congregation is true to the Lord, but part of my tithe goes to support apostate teachers. I'm rethinking my pledge to the Lord.

Did you find your church, here?

#   #   #   #

Maurice (Maury) A. Johnson

Future History

A capsule view

Maurice (Maury) A. Johnson

———END OF THE LINE!

This Musing will begin a series that will enlighten us as to future history. I've studied this subject of prophesy for nearly 40 years and the future is clearly outlined in the teachings of Jesus and the prophets. I would like to make it very clear that I am a student of eschatology and not a prophet.

Nearly 23% of the Bible tells about future happenings and yes, it is the most neglected portion of God's Word. One of the reasons for the neglect is our dependence on the old biblical students for knowledge. Yet, the Bible tells us that we won't know much about it until the last days. Those last days are fast approaching! Predicted events are coming fast and furious.

Please bear with me as I attempt to cover subjects deserving of six volumes in a whole lot less words. I am not a preacher who would cover each of the following three ways to make sure you understood them. I was a technical writer and a audio-visual producer in my working world. I will muse on the following nine themes.

(1)   End-times
(2)   The rapture
(3)   The Tribulation, the first half
(4)   The Tribulation Church
(5)   The Third Temple
(6)   The Tribulation, the last half
(7)   Armageddon
(8)   The Millennium
(9)   After the Millennium

I will print out some of the important references and list others but I cannot list all in this space. I have no intention of just writing a long bibliography.

# # # #

————END-TIMES

> *And he said, "Go your way, Daniel, for these*
> *words are concealed and sealed up until the*
> *end of time." (Dan. 12:9)*
> *"But as for you, Daniel, conceal these words*
> *and seal up the book until the end of time;*
> *many will go back and forth, and knowledge*
> *will increase." (Dan. 12:4)*

Now we know why Augustine and Luther couldn't get it right. They were born centuries too soon! Consider this for the knowledge part of verse 4. Science tells us that all the lore from Adam's day until 1986, doubled in the next six years. The doubling rate of knowledge is now 19-20 months. Most of that is due to computers like the one I am writing on now.

My first trip to Europe took me near three weeks in a B-17. I have made it in 10 hours to London from Seattle and SSTs have done it in about four hours, New York to London. It looks like the transportation requirement is fulfilled.

Many times, the nation of Israel is referred to as "the fig tree" in prophesy. One of the end-times signs, is the return of the Jews from the diaspora, or scattering.

> *"Now learn the parable from the fig*
> *tree: when it's branch has become*
> *tender, and puts forth it's*
> *leaves, you know that summer is near:*
> *even so you, too, when you see all these*

> *things, recognize that He is near, right at the door." Truly I say to you, this generation will not pass away until all these things take place." (Matt. 24:32,33,34)*

Even though Jews arrive in Israel from many generations of being absorbed into foreign cultures, they still meld into Israeli society because of their customs and the Yiddish language. From Russia, Ethiopia, the Orient and the rest of the world they have come to the land God has promised them. In Musings to come, we will see that the title to that land does not come easy!

#   #   #   #

END-TIMES

Then He continued by saying to them, "Nation shall rise against nation, and kingdom against kingdom, and there will be great earthquakes, and in various places plagues and famines, and there will be terrors and great signs from heaven." (Luke 21:10,11)

That nation against nation should really be translated *ethnic group against ethnic group.* We can't argue with the Lord, we are seeing that happen all over the globe. From Bosnia to the Sudan, Afghanistan to Iran and even in South America it's happening.

We now have more than six billion people on this earth and we are putting a strain on the resources God gave us, thus the famines and we are seeing them all over the world.

The AIDS plague is a natural consequence of our failure to heed some of our creator's no-nos. AIDS began in West Africa and was first known as the "Green Monkey" disease. I am told that there are more than 230 venereal diseases for the promiscuous.

Bin Laden's school for terrorists are killing off thousands. We hear about the plane-loads of people he kills and the buildings he brings down. We don't hear about the Near East havoc he wreaks.

"And in various places there will be famines and earthquakes." (Matt.24: 7b)

329

Maurice (Maury) A. Johnson

Scientists call a trembler of 5.8 on the Richter scale a killer quake. Very rare before 1930, the earth's plates have recently been slipping at a near exponential rate.

> *Just as there will also be false teachers among*
> *you even denying the Master who bought them,*
> *bringing swift destruction upon themselves.*
> *(2 Peter 2:1b)*

I am very sorry have to tell you that many mainline churches are being infiltrated by false teachers. (Matt. 24:11) The powers-to-be, Cardinals, Bishops and councils are bowing to political pressures and going against God's words.

> *Do not be deceived, "God is not mocked; for*
> *whatever a man sows, this he will also reap."*
> *(Gal. 6:7)*

\#   \#   \#   \#

———THE RAPTURE

The word "rapture" is not found in the Bible. It is from the Greek and it means transportation to another place or sphere of existence. Unlike many other events of the end times, there is nothing prophesied that must happen before the rapture takes place!

> *"And He will send forth His angels with a great trumpet and they will gather together His elect from the four winds, from one end of the sky to the other." (Matt. 24:31)*

The timing of the rapture has long been a matter of conjecture. We know this! We know that we will be gone from this earth before God's wrath falls upon this planet. We are told this several times. (Rom. 5:9, 1 Thess. 5:9, I Thess. 1:10)

The angel Gabriel instructed Daniel as to end-days events. (Dan. 9:27) He told of 70 weeks (of years) until the end of man's reign. The first 69 weeks (483 years) were fulfilled to the day with the crucifixion of our Lord. Then there is a gap of approximately 2000 years while He builds His church. The 70th week of 7 years begins with the Antichrist signing a peace pact with Israel. (Dan. 9:27) Thus begins seven years of tribulation! We are told the length of the Tribulation in days, months and years!

David's interpretation of king Nebuchadnezzar's dreams tells us that the Roman Empire will rise again. Out of this empire, a terrible dictator will rise. He is the Antichrist! We don't hear much about the European Union (EU) on this side of the ocean, but it or it's successor will be the revived Roman Empire!

No warning! Our Lord has warned us that the rapture can occur at any time. We are to be ready like the ten virgins for that trumpet call at all times. (*Matt. 25:1-13*) The church will become the bride of Christ after the rapture.

> *"Let us rejoice and be glad and give the glory to Him for the marriage of the Lamb has come and His bride has made herself ready." And it was given to her to clothe herself in fine linen, bright and clean; for the fine linen is the righteous acts of the saints. (Rev. 19:7,8)*

———THE RAPTURE

The church at Thessalonica got some bum dope about the rapture and the members were worried that the Day of the Lord had come and left them behind. Paul straightened them out with his second letter to them. Here, I make my case for a pre-tribulation rapture.

> *Let no one in any way deceive you, for it will not come unless the apostasy comes first, and the man of lawlessness is revealed, the son of destruction, (2 Thess. 2:3)*

Of course, the man of lawlessness is the Antichrist, but, we will be gone before he is revealed!

> *And you know what restrains him now, so that in his time he may be revealed. For the mystery of lawlessness is already at work; only he who now restrains will do so until he is taken out of the way. And then that lawless one will be revealed whom the Lord will slay with the breath of His mouth and bring to an end by the appearance of His coming:*
> *(2 Thess. 2:6-8)*

Who is the restrainer? Some think it's a person or a political system. I say it has to be the Holy Spirit who is in the believer! God will never completely desert the earth, but we believers will via the rapture. I can see no other who can fill the bill of restrainer!

Remember, there is no specific event in prophesy that must be fulfilled before the rapture. Remember this, at the rapture, we will rise to meet the Lord in the clouds. At Armageddon, he will come to the earth. Onward and upward!'

#   #   #   #

———THE TRIBULATION (The first half)

The Lord is slow to anger and great in power,
and the Lord will by no means leave the guilty
unpunished. (Nahum 1:3)

We are anxious to tell of God's great love for us but we tend to forget that He will get angry. We marvel that He would sacrifice His own Son so that we wouldn't have to go to Hell, but could come to live with Him at the end of man's reign on earth. His soon to arrive anger is called the Tribulation. He gives all a last chance to get a free passport to Heaven.

"The Lord is not slow about His promise, as
some count slowness, but is patient toward
you, not wishing for any to perish but for all to
come to repentance." (2 Peter 3:9)

Last call, folks! Even when God gets mad, He gives everyone a last minute chance. For those who missed the first flight to Heaven, there is one more chance.

As I mentioned earlier, the Tribulation starts the moment the Antichrist signs a peace pact with Israel. It lasts seven years and ends at Armageddon. During this era, there will be wars, droughts, great epidemics, anarchy and murders galore. It will be a terrible time to be on earth with the believers gone.

One of the wars that will take place is the Magog war. Russia and friends, Iran, Iraq, Libya and others will attack little old Israel. They will get their comeuppance as God shows some of His anger.

> Speaking to Russia and friends. *"You shall fall on the mountains of Israel, you and all your troops, and the peoples who are with you; (Ezek.39:4)*

Even the homeland of the former Communist country isn't spared as God gets revenge for all the atrocities the USSR has committed.

> *"And I shall send fire upon Magog and those who inhabit the coastlands in safety; and they will know that I am the Lord. (Ezek. 39:6)*

As we will see, the Tribulation has a real socko ending, but first—

———THE TRIBULATION (First half)

One good thing that happens at this time is that the Lord reveals Himself to His chosen people, Israel.

> *"And I will not hide My face from them any longer, for I shall have poured out My Spirit on the house of Israel," declares the Lord God. (Ezek. 39:29)*

At the midpoint of the tribulation, the Antichrist who has assumed the throne of the revised Roman Empire, declares he is to be worshiped and seats himself in the temple. He now has control of most of Europe and much of Asia. He sets up an economic system using computer chips or a bar code in or on everyone's right hand or forehead. It is needed before anyone can buy or sell! (*Rev. 13:16*)

> *Here is wisdom. Let him who has understanding calculate the number of the beast, for the number is that of a man; and his number is six hundred and sixty-six. (Rev. 13:18)*

Ah, here is a mystery. Many people have tried to figure out who the Antichrist is. If you can puzzle it out, let me know. Hint: in both of the Hebrew and Greek alphabets, each letter has a number equivalent.

Despite the fact that the real church is gone and only a false church is still on the earth, many will remember the gospel they heard before and didn't accept. Many of them

337

will seek the Lord's forgiveness and most, if not all, will be martyred for that faith.

> *And when He broke the fifth seal, I saw underneath the altar the souls of those who had been slain because of the word of God, and because of the testimony which they had maintained. (Rev. 6:9)*

THE TRIBULATION (the first half)

Much of the bad stuff is taking Place in or around Israel. Jesus warns the Israelis to flee and seek a refuge when the Antichrist declares himself to be God.

> *"Therefore when you see the Abomination of Desolation which was spoken of through Daniel the prophet, standing in the holy place then let those who are in Judea flee to the mountains; let him who is on the housetop not go down to get the things out that are in his house:" (Matt. 24:15-17)*

If you read on in Chapter 24, you'll see that those who escape will have to make a speedy exit. Many of us believe that Petra will be their place of refuge. Petra is a city of thousands of caves that are cut into rock cliffs. This fortress is in SW Jordan. It has been stocked with food and items necessary for life by American Jews. Petra is included in many holy land tours.

Everything comes to a halt while 144,000 Jews become believers and are sealed with the Lord's sign. (Rev. 7:1-8) God resurrects two witnesses. (I think they will be Moses and Elijah) They will preach for 3 1/2 years before they are killed. Their bodies lay in the street for for 3 1/2 days. A great earthquake happens as they arise and are taken to Heaven. I wonder if it will be seen on CNN.

Things do not go well for the Antichrist in Jerusalem where he has set up his capitol. The daughter of the king of the South fails in a peace initiative and he has a small war on his hands. He barely squeaks out of that and he gets word of a 200 million man/woman army coming from the Orient. By the way, China has bragged that they can field 200 million soldiers by themselves.

Well, things are not quite set up for Armageddon, but let's take a look at the church of the Tribulation. The last half of the Tribulation is known as the Great Tribulation.

#   #   #   #

———CHURCH OF THE TRIBULATION

Well, the real church is gone but there is a false one to take it's place. It's hard for many of us to understand, but church-goers are not always Christians. As we will see, even some of the leaders don't belong to the Lord. Let's consider the basics.

> *"For God so loved the world, that He gave His only begotten Son, that whoever believes in Him should not perish, but have eternal life.(John 3:16)*

Then, we pray for wisdom, and with wisdom, understanding.

> *"Trust in the Lord with all your heart, and do not lean on your own understanding, in all your ways acknowledge Him. And He will make your paths straight." (Prov. 3:5)*

That sounds like the way to wisdom! Let's pursue it further.

> *All scripture is inspired by God and profitable for teaching, for reproof, for correction, for training in righteousness: (2 Tim. 3:16)*

Here is where a lot of denomination and church leaders go wrong.

> *Be diligent to present yourself approved to God, a worker who does not need to be ashamed, rightly dividing the word of truth. (2 Tim. 2:15)*

Our Lord tells us to expect false christs and false teachers in the last days and there are many of them. A great many of them are pretenders who have infiltrated the churches. A lot are political animals who want to please everyone. One major denomination has removed Christ as the only way to salvation from it's constitution. It's General Assembly calls Jesus "unique," but does not affirm He is Lord alone. All denominations are under attack by those who wrongly divide the word of truth. Satan is having a hey-day in all of the major denominations and churches. This deviance from God's truth is called the apostasy.

CHURCH OF THE TRIBULATION-2

Just as the real church of Jesus Christ is made up of people from every Christian denomination, the false church will be also. I have been a student of human nature for 76 years and permit me an observation. I believe that many of the powers-that-be who miss the rapture, Cardinals, Bishops, Councilmen and Leaders, will not give up their positions of power. They will stay with the ship and go to Hell with it. Harsh words? Yep!

In the first three chapters of Revelation, Christ Himself reviews the condition of seven churches in Turkey. These congregations represent the ones that exist today as well as the church through the ages. Five of the seven have failed in some way! Generally it is (was) due to false leaders and prophets. There will be those who overcome in all the churches.

> *He who has an ear, let him hear what the Spirit says to the churches.*
> *"He who overcomes shall not be hurt by the second death." (Rev. 2:11)*

I have sensed for many years that this false church will be an amalgamation of many denominations. Years ago, I had thought that the consolidation into a unified grouping would be brought about by the World Council of Churches. I never in my wildest dreams guessed that the mainline churches would forsake solid doctrine for the purpose of unification. Just like the nations that clump together during the Tribulation, the church leaders falsely think "bigger is better."

How about the leader of the false church? Pope John Paul 2 believes that his successor will be the Antichrist. He says that he has Cardinals that don't believe in the virgin birth! He cannot be right about a pope being the Antichrist. His candidate however could be the religious leader (The False Prophet) who aids the Antichrist. Satan mimics the triune God with himself, the Antichrist and the religious leader. (False Prophet)

The ancient city, Babylon has been a thorn in God's side since the days of the Tower of Babel. It is the "cradle of democracy" according to Saddam Hussein. It is also the birthplace of all of the false religions of the world. According to my dictionary, the name Babylon is used to describe cities of luxury. Apparently, in the 17th chapter of Revelation, the whole economic/religious system gets it's due. It is truly the time of God's wrath!

———CHURCH OF THE TRIBULATION

The pretender church of this era is identified as a woman, the mother of harlots and the abominations of the earth. (Rev. 17:5)

I saw the woman drunk with the blood of the saints and with the blood of the martyrs of Jesus. (Rev. 17:6a)

Evidently, the church is responsible for martyring those that come to Christ during this time. The church headquarters will be in Rome.

"Here is the mind which has wisdom: The seven heads are seven mountains on which the woman sits." (Rev. 17:9)

Apparently, the churches that are hell-bent *(the right words)* on unifying today will be together under one head during the Tribulation. The member nations get tired of the woman and destroy her. (Rev. 18:8) Things are nearly ready for the big war!

#   #   #   #

Maurice (Maury) A. Johnson

────THE TEMPLE

Orthodox Jews have been looking forward to having a temple in which to make sacrifices to Jehovah.   For centuries, they have longed to bring animals to be sacrificed for sin atonement.   They will get their wish.   We don't know when it will start, but the third temple will be completed by the mid-point of the seven-year Tribulation when the Antichrist takes it over.

> *Who opposes and exalts himself above every*
> *so-called god or object of worship, so that he*
> *takes his seat in the temple of God, displaying*
> *himself as being God (2 Thess. 4)*

Before any construction begins, a great many things must be done.   Plans must be drawn and the site must be prepared.   With   the   temple,   there   are   even   more considerations that are necessary.   Let's take a look at what we know.

The plans are done?   It surprised me to learn that electrical schematics are included!   A big problem is with the siting of the building.   The Muslim Dome of the Rock occupies the mountaintop where the temple is to go.   Of course, the Muslims resist even the explorations by rabbis in the tunnels under the Temple Mount.   We know that the destruction of the second temple was complete as Jesus predicted. (*Matt 24:2*) He didn't say that the huge foundation stones would be moved and the siting committee believes the Temple can be built without displacing the Dome of the Rock!

Many necessary items for the sacrifice are being completed. Bronze lavers for the ceremonial washing are being finished. Robes for the Levites are being sewn and dyed. Here, the tailors faced some difficulty. A search finally found the source of a purple dye needed for those robes. It was a small seashell found in the Mediterranean Sea. Another glitch was finding a pure red heifer that will be burnt and its ashes used to consecrate the altar. A pure strain of cattle has been found and the breeding program is under way.

Found and lost! The Jews finally get their temple and then when the Antichrist takes over they have to flee for their lives! (*Matt. 24:15-17*) When he seats himself in the temple, it's known as the abomination of desolation.

#   #   #   #

———THE TRIBULATION (Last half)

This one is not easy to write about. I know that we believers will be gone before God's wrath comes to the earth. I know, too, that He has given everyone every chance to accept His grace. The second shoe is about to fall! The last half of the Tribulation is due!

Leading up to the great last war are seven bowl judgements. (*Rev. chap. 16*) These woes are more terrible than anything in the past. Consider these things!

(1.) Loathsome sores on those who took the mark of the beast! (*Staph infection?*)

(2.) All sea creatures die!

(3.) Fresh water no longer potable.

(4.) Terrible sunburns ensue. (*Ozone layer gone?*)

(5.) Pains and sores and darkness. (*Nuclear night?*)

(6.) The Euphrates River is stopped at the Ataturk Dam, allowing the army of the East to march to Israel. Turkey brags about being able to shut the river off for eight months.

(7.) The mother of all earthquakes levels mountains and sinks islands. Jerusalem splits into three parts. The great cities of the world are destroyed. Hailstones of 100 pounds pelt the earth after nuclear explosions. The woes are confirmed in the fourteenth chapter of Zephaniah. This is how neutron bombs affect people.

> *Now this will be the plague with which the Lord will strike all the peoples who have gone to war against Jerusalem; their flesh will rot while they stand on their feet, and their eyes*

*will rot in their sockets, and their tongue will
rot in their mouth. (Zech. 14:12)*

All the world's armies are now gathered near the city of
Megiddo.

#   #   #   #

———ARMAGEDDON

The Lord tells us that if He didn't put an end to things, no one would be left alive!

> *Then I saw heaven opened and a white horse standing there; and the one sitting on the horse was named "Faithful and True"—the one who justly punishes and makes war. (Rev. 19:11)*

All the world's armies are gathered in and around Israel. They were gathered at the urging of Satan for a last-ditch battle against God. There are a great many, 200 million soldiers from the Orient alone. (*Rev. 9:16)*

> *And the rest were killed with the sword which came from the mouth of Him who sat upon the horse, and all the birds were filled with their flesh. (Rev. 19:21)*

Millions of dead bodies litter the battlefield. The appetites of the carrion eaters are sated as they tear the flesh of generals and soldiers alike. We are told that the blood runs five feet deep for 200 miles. (Rev. *14:20)*

A tour of the battlefield shows that tanks, helicopters, trucks and other war machinery lay stilled as far as the eye can see. They will never be used for purposes of war again!

In an early judgement, the Antichrist and the religious leader are sent to the Lake of Fire and there they will be tormented forever. Satan is seized and chained up for a thousand years.   Those that accepted the Lord's grace during the Tribulation join us in Heaven. (*Rev. 20:4*)

We believers have come back with the Lord. We are wearing white linen, not bulletproof vests. (*Rev. 19:14*) We have work to do, but first, we'll praise the King of Kings and Lord of Lords. Next, the Millennium.

#   #   #   #

——THE MILLENNIUM

The King is here! The Creator is creating again after His 6,000 year "day" of rest. The earth is a mess after all the wars, epidemics and catastrophes and we have work to do!

There are people in their natural bodies who survived the Tribulation but not near the population of six billion plus the earth holds as I write this. The birds of prey and the carrion eaters are taking care of the dead flesh. Bulldozers will be burying the bones for seven months. The instruments of war become instruments of peace.

The leadership of the world is completely different. Jesus is King over all the Universe. David is King of the Jews (Ezek. 27:24) and the disciples are each over one of the tribes of Israel. (Matt. 19:28-30) How about you and me?

> *Do you not know that the saints will judge the world?*
> *And if the world be judged by you, are you unworthy to judge the smallest matters? Do you not know that we shall judge angels?*
> *(! Cor. 6:2,3)*

We will definitely not spend our days laying around on a cloud all day plucking harp strings. God gave us talents before we were born and gifts when we became His. We'll use them. There will have to be Kings, Governors, mayors and other officials as well as judges over the nations. Nations refers to gentile countries.

352

I said that God will create again. lie will restore the earth to where it was when Adam was made from dust. (*Rev. 22:3*) The ages of those peoples in their earthly bodies will be what they were before the flood. (*lsa. 65:20*) Even the wild animals will not be a threat as they will be converted to plant eaters and the snakes will lose their venom. (*Isa. 65:24:25*) Science tells us that species of flora and fauna are going extinct at a alarming rate. They will all be back. Biologists will have a ball!

We are told that we will have the same properties that our Savior had after His resurrection. That means we will be able to buzz about the universe at the speed of thought. You can zip through walls. You'll think you are Superman.

——THE MIILLENNIUM (Cont.)

I had written that the saints will hold the positions of responsibility here on earth. In addition to talent, there are other qualifications for the job. We are not told that neatness counts, but *faithfulness* while we were on earth does! So does service. (*Luke 22:24*)

> *His lord said to him, Well done, good and faithful servant, you were faithful over a few things, I will make you a ruler over many things. Enter into the joy of your Lord."* (*Matt; 25:21*)

Throughout the centuries, mankind has tried many kinds of governments, from kingdoms to communism to capitalism. All have attempted to find Utopia and failed. Here we have it as good as it gets while we still have human beings around. The one coming next will be perfection.

What could you do if you didn't have any phobias, inhibitions or worldly junk on your brain? Back at the rapture when your sanctification was complete those things were gone! Think of all the accomplishments that will be made during this time. None of them will have anything to do with war! (*Micah 4:3, Isa. 2:4*)

The leftover weapons of war furnish the power needs for Israel for seven years. With the plutonium, oil and the gasoline from the battlefield, Israel has no dependence on Arabic.

"They will not take wood from the field nor cut down any from the forests, because they will make fires with the weapons." (Ezek. 39:10)

This is a time of prosperity like nothing ever seen before! Israel will be especially blessed as they apply God's rules for farming. Farmers won't even have to contend with weeds.

Here, I want to emphasize that we saints are not subject to the things that govern the people who are in their old earthly bodies. We saints are sons/daughters of God. All our needs are taken care of by our Father! No, we won't have to fret about insurance, or money, or doctors, or rent, or grocery bills. None of these things will exist for saints. Thanks be to God!

———THE MILLENNIUM (Cont.)

Sometime, either during the millennium or shortly after, we will move our residence. We believers will have a new address. I don't know the street names, but the city's name is the New Jerusalem. It is made of pure, translucent gold and has giant pearls for gates. The city is 1,500 miles wide, 1,500 miles deep and 1,500 miles high. It will come down from heaven. It's lavishly decorated with jewels as you would expect from the Master Creator. Most importantly, it contains our Father God and His Son, our Savior, Who will live with us. Read Rev, oh. 21,22.

There is trouble in paradise. Satan is released at the end of a thousand years to deceive "who he may" of those who are still in earthly bodies. *(Rev. 20:7-10)* The old rabble-rouser finds rebels to mount an offensive against God. They surround Jerusalem and God zaps them with fire. This time, Satan is gone for good. He is thrown into the Lake of Fire where the Antichrist and the Religious Leader (False Prophet) already reside. There is no escape!

Also at the Millennium end comes judgement day. At this judgement day, the dead who are not in Christ are raised and are the only participants. They are from ancient days, through the ages and even from the Millennium rebellion. None can say they never got the Word. For each one, the verdict is "Guilty." The Lake of Fire is final. For some, the punishment there will be tougher than others, but it is forever! *(Luke 12:47,48)*

#   #   #   #

——AFTER THE MILLENNIUM

Well, the sheep and the goats have been separated and the goats are gone. The sinners are in the Lake of Fire and we are living in God's house. There is no church, temple or synagogue, for our Creator and Savior are living with us! (Rev. 21:22)

I get a mixed message as to when we move into the New Jerusalem. Chronologically, it would seem to follow the millennium. We are told that no sin will enter in which would place it during the millennium when people in natural bodies are still present. Although I introduced the beautiful city during the millennium, I'll do it again.

> *Now I saw a new heaven and a new earth, for the first heaven and the first earth had passed away. Also there was no more sea. Then I, John, saw the holy city, New Jerusalem, coming down out of heaven from God, prepared as a bride adorned for her husband (Rev. 21:1,2)*

I suspect that the earth will be cleansed with fire so that no trace of sin will ever be found. (Rev. 21:1) No future archaeologist will ever dig up an object of worship from a sinful world.

> *"And He shall wipe away every tear from their eyes; and there shall no longer be any death; and there shall no longer be any mourning, or*

Maurice (Maury) A. Johnson

> *crying, or pain; the first things have passed away." (Rev. 21:4)*

I do hope that the Lord will allow me tears of joy. I have those now when I contemplate the wonders He has prepared for me.

# # # #

ABOUT THE AUTHOR

Maury Johnson fancies himself as a hometown humorist and poor man's philosopher. He began his Musings as a mini-lesson for his church's newsletter in 1984. The Musings are now a staple in other newsletters. The other chapters, Seven Churches, Heavenly Days and Future History, are a result of his 40 years of end-days prophesy study.

Most of his workaday world was spent in the engineering fields and as a technical writer-photographer for audio-visual films for under-water weaponry. Nearly all of it was for the U.S. Navy. You won't find any church-speak because he dislikes jargon with a purple passion.

Maury is a veteran of World War II where he served as a gunner in B17 Flying Fortresses in the air over Europe. He was awarded the Air Medal and several other medals for his service. After discharge at wars end, he was lured into the Naval Air Reserve to backseat Helldiver dive bombers. In his 22 reserve years, he served as first crew Flight Engineer and Leading Chief of a patrol squadron.

He and Happy-Toes pledged their troth in 1944. She says it was September 5th and he says the 7th, so they celebrate on different days to the amusement of the four kids, ten grandchildren and four great-grandkids. The family is extremely close and all except two grandchildren live in the same county. Maury donates time as a Senior Volunteer Policeman in his hometown of Poulsbo, Washington. He's volunteered with Scouts, peewee sports, church and civic programs. A former fisherman, camper and hunter, his tired legs now keep him close to home.

Although Maury wrote short story humor at one time, he now does his writing for the Lord.

Printed in the United States
24969LVS00001B/234

9 781418 437282